PRAYERS
ENCIRCLING
THE
WORLD

PRAYERS ENCIRCLING THE WORLD

An International Anthology

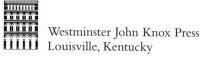

Westminster John Knox Press
Louisville, Kentucky

Cover illustration by Emma Whiting

First published in 1998 by SPCK.
Reprinted by arrangement with SPCK, Great Britain.

First American Edition, 1999
Published by Westminster John Knox Press
Louisville, Kentucky

This book is printed on acid-free paper that meets the American National Standards Institute Z39.48 standard. ♾

PRINTED IN THE UNITED STATES OF AMERICA

99 00 01 02 03 04 05 06 07 08 – 10 9 8 7 6 5 4 3 2

Library of Congress Cataloging-in-Publication Data
Prayers encircling the world : an international anthology.
    p.   cm.
Includes indexes.
ISBN 0-664-25821-2 (alk. paper)
    1. Prayers.   I. Westminster John Knox Press.
BV245.P825   1999
242'.8—dc21   98-53720

CONTENTS

1 Jesus,
light of our hearts,
since your resurrection,
you always come to us.
Whatever point we may be at,
you are always waiting for us.
And you tell us:
Come to me,
you who are overburdened,
and you will find relief.

Brother Roger of Taizé, France

PRAISE TO GOD

We have heard about you, *1*　　　　　　　　　　　　2
God of all power.
You made the world out of kindness,
creating order out of confusion;
you made each one of us in your own image;
your fingerprint is on every soul.
So we praise you.
We praise and worship you.

We have heard about you,
Jesus Christ:
the carpenter who left his tools and trade;
the poor man who made others rich;
the healer who let himself be wounded;
the criminal on whom the soldiers spat
not knowing they were fouling the face of God;
the saviour who died and rose again.
So we praise you.
We praise and worship you.

We have heard about you,
Holy Spirit.
You broke the bonds of every race and nation,
to let God speak in every tongue;
you made disciples drunk with grace;
you converted souls and emptied pockets;
you showed how love made all things new
and opened the doors to change and freedom.
So we praise you.
We praise and worship you.

Iona Community, Scotland

3   Great Spirit, piler up of rocks into towering mountains! When you stamp on the stone, the dust rises and fills the land. Hardness of the precipice; waters of the flood that turn into misty rain when stirred. Vessel overflowing with oil! Father who sews the heavens like cloth: let him knit together that which is below. Caller-forth of the branching trees, you bring forth the shoots that stand erect. You have filled the land with people; the dust rises on high, O Lord! Wonderful one, you live in the midst of the sheltering rocks. You give rain to humankind. Hear us, O Lord! Show mercy when we beg you, O Lord! You are on high with the spirits of the great. You raise the grass-covered hills above the earth, and create the rivers, Gracious One!

Shona people, Zimbabwe

4   To you, God of creation, we sing a new song of praise.
        A song of trees planted by streams of living water,
        a song of mountains clapping their hands for joy,
        a song of cities delighting in heavenly harmony,
        a song of people that were lost and have been found.
        For the earth is the Lord's and we shall be glad in it.
        Hallelujah.

The people of Pitt Street Uniting Church, Sydney, Australia

We thank you, Lord,   5
whose finger touched our dust,
who gave us breath.

We thank you, Lord,
who gave us sight and sense
to see the flowers,
to hear the wind,
to feel the waters in our hand,

To sleep with the night
and wake with the sun,
to stand upon this earth,
to hear your voice,
to sing your praise.

Our hearts are stirred
with each new sight and sound.

Like a stream
the whole world pours into our lives,
and eyes, and hands,

And fills our souls
with the joy of gratitude
and living gladness.

We want to embrace
and experience and express
every good thing in your world.

O Lord our God,
how excellent is your name.

Terry C Falla, Australia

7

6   Lord, Holy Spirit,
you blow like the wind in a thousand paddocks.
Inside and outside the fences,
you blow where you wish to blow.

Lord, Holy Spirit,
you are the sun who shines on the little plant.
You warm him gently, you give him life,
you raise him up to become a tree with many leaves.

Lord, Holy Spirit,
you are the mother eagle with her young,
holding them in peace under your feathers.
On the highest mountain you have built your nest,
above the valley, above the storms of the world,
where no hunter ever comes.

Lord, Holy Spirit,
you are the bright cloud in whom we hide,
in whom we know already that the battle has been won.
You bring us to our Brother Jesus,
to rest our heads upon his shoulder.

Lord, Holy Spirit,
in the love of friends you are building a new house.
Heaven is with us when you are with us.
You are singing your song in the hearts of the poor.
Guide us, wound us, heal us. Bring us to God.

James K Baxter, Aotearoa (New Zealand)

Bright and beautiful God, 7
thank you for our world,
a place full of beauty and variety.
Thank you for the wind and the waves,
the stars in the sky, the changing of the seasons,
the animals in all their splendour.

Thank you, God, for the gift of people,
men, women and children,
of many colours and creeds,
in different shapes and sizes,
with many gifts and talents,
all made and loved by you.

Thank you, God, for the variety of life;
everything points to your love and glory.

Francis Brienen, United Kingdom

We are thankful, O God, for the door of your grace which makes 8
us sharers in your Kingdom. God of all, we thank you for the
opportunity which you offer us every single day to open ourselves
to your Spirit, to delight in you and to serve you in newness of life.

Women's World Day of Prayer, 1988

9   O my Father, Great Elder,
          I have no words to thank you,
          but with your deep wisdom
          I am sure that you can see
          how I value your glorious gifts.
          O my Father, when I look upon your greatness,
          I am overcome with awe.
          O Great Elder,
          ruler of all things on earth and in heaven,
          I am your warrior,
          ready to act according to your will.

          Kikuyu people, Kenya

10   O thou Chief of Chiefs, we kneel before thee in obeisance and
     adoration. Like the bird in the branches, we praise thy heavenly
     glory. Like the village sharpening stone, thou art always available
     and never exhausted. Remove, we pray thee, our sins that hide thy
     face. Thou knowest that we are poor and unlearned; that we often
     work when hungry. Send rain in due season for our gardens that
     our food may not fail. Protect us from the cold and danger by night.
     Help us to keep in health that we may rejoice in strength. May our
     villages be filled with children. Emancipate us from the fear of the
     fetish and the witch doctor and from all manner of superstitions. Save
     the people, especially the Christian boys and girls in the villages,
     from the evil that surrounds them. All this we ask in the name of
     Jesus Christ thy Son.

          Unknown writer, Zaire

Blessed be your name, O most blessed giver of seasons.　　11
This autumn evening is your gift;
　　the gentle air caresses our faces,
　　the scent of soil after rain
　　is fragrant in our nostrils,
　　the body relaxes,
　　and the mind absorbs the quiet of dusk.
The meal time is over,
　　children have ceased their games and gone inside,
　　and the birds have ended their songs –
except for the evening call
　　of a lone wagtail from a jacaranda tree.
Above and beyond our planet,
the velvet flanks of space
　　begin to glisten with the light of stars
supported by a thin crescent of light from a young moon.

This evening, Lord,
our praise rises as simply and sweetly
as the call of that lone wagtail.

'It is good to give thanks to the Lord,
to sing songs of your love, most loving one!
To affirm your presence in the morning,
and at evening to sing of your love,
to pluck the strings of the guitar,
to give melody to the flute
and make harmony on the harp.
Your deeds, O Lord, fill me with gladness;
your gifts move me to songs of joy.'
Hallelujah!

Bruce D Prewer, Australia

12   Praise the name of the Lord
Praise God who has given us hope!
Praise God, you people living in the land of South Africa
in the streets and farms of our God.

From high blue skies to hot deep mines
from dusty deserts to towering peaks
from grey littered streets to green fields and forests,
From oceans edged with warm white beaches
to concrete cities and long black highways:
The Lord's will is sovereign.

Sing glory to the name of God who inspires hope
Because God has called South Africa to be saved.
We have learned for ourselves that God is great,
that our Lord surpasses all other gods.

The Lord struck down the idols of apartheid,
and denounced pride and racism.
The Lord sent signs and wonders against the false gospel,
and forced change upon its officials . . .

O Lord, your name endures for ever!
Lord, your memory is ever fresh.
For you have vindicated your children
And honoured those who served God's people.

South Africa Council of Churches

Our Pacific islands are yours, O Lord,   13
and all the seas that surround them.
You made the palm trees grow,
and the birds fly in the air.

When we see your beautiful rising sun
and hear the waves splash on our shores,
when we see the new moon rise
and the old moon sink,

We know, O Lord, how wonderful you are.
You bless our people;
from Truk to Tonga and beyond
you spread your caring wings.

Even when we sail through stormy seas,
and fly amidst rain clouds,
we know you await us,
with kaikai and coconut.

You who turn storms into gentle winds,
and troubled seas into tranquil waters,
you who make yams grow
and bananas blossom,

Wash our people with justice;
teach us with righteousness;
speak to us daily;
strengthen us to serve you.

Bernard Narakobi, Papua New Guinea

14   Thank you, O Lord our God, for all that you have done to
sustain us.
Here in the Caribbean there are so many things that give
us pleasure:
beaches, mountains, valleys, trees, fruits and flowers.
Indeed, all nature celebrates you in this part of your creation.
Thank you for the people who dwell in our territories,
that in them we see a reflection of all the races of the world.
Thank you for your beloved Son Jesus Christ;
for his life, his mission, his teaching, his sufferings,
his death and resurrection;
And that this Jesus who is our Saviour, lives today.

Caribbean Conference of Churches

WORSHIP

Come among us, living Lord,   15
we come to hear your living word.
We meet together in the name of Christ
to share your mission and your sacrifice;
to receive the power which only you can give,
    that we might live!
Come fill this time of silence.

Martin John Nicholls, United Kingdom

O Lord, our heavenly Father, the giver of all good gifts, we praise   16
and thank you for all your blessings to us. Forgive us that so often
we are more ready to turn to you in times of trouble and need
rather than to thank you in the good times. No matter what happens to us, teach us to be thankful. Help us not to take for granted
your gift of life itself; our health and strength; the love and support
of family and friends; the beauty of your creation. Above all, thank
you for your greatest gift – the way of forgiveness you have provided by sending your Son to be our Saviour.

You give us so much, dear Lord. Help us to give you something
in return – the love of our hearts, a willingness to serve you and to
share your love with others. Grant us day by day a true spirit of
thankfulness.

Jean Fenton, Ireland

17 O God, we have come together in prayer, knowing that you are present in our midst. We wish to know you better and worship you with joy. We offer ourselves to be your servants and to be good neighbours to one another. We trust in you with all our heart. We praise you for all you have done for us. We are happy that we are together in this worship service. We believe in the power of prayer and its ability to call everyone to fullness of life. Jesus, fill us with your love. We belong to you today, tomorrow and for ever.

Women's World Day of Prayer, 1988,
written by women from Madagascar

18 Thank you, Lord God, our heavenly Father, that you are always merciful to us. Thank you that you have created us in your own image so that we may love you, glorify you and serve you. Thank you for many blessings you give us day by day: food, clothing, shelter, children, partners, friends, rainfall, sunshine, changes of weather, winter, summer, spring and autumn. All these and many other graces show us how great and merciful you are to us, your children. We are sinners, who do not deserve such blessings. But since you are merciful, kind and just, you provide these things without any cost.

Thank you also that you have revealed yourself to us through Jesus Christ your dear Son, who came on this earth and died for our sins. Thank you that you have sent us your Holy Spirit so that he may guide us in our Christian paths. We ask you to continue to bless us day by day, and give us courage, hope and strength so that we may continue to follow and serve you faithfully.

We ask all this through Jesus Christ, our Lord and Saviour.

Sylvester T Kafunzile, Tanzania

God, give us a new heart,   19
big enough to love;
God, give us a new heart,
strong enough to fight.

Renewed people, creators of history –
builders of a new humanity;
renewed people who live with adventure
as they go on their long pilgrimage:
God, give us a new heart,
big enough to love.

Renewed people, struggling in hope –
thirsty pilgrims, seeking truth and light;
renewed people, now free from all their chains –
freedom-loving people, demanding liberty:
God, give us a new heart,
strong enough to fight.

Renewed people, loving without limit –
without regard to race or pride of place;
renewed people, standing by the poor –
sharing with them their homes and their bread.
God, give us a new heart,
big enough to love,
strong enough to fight.

Unknown poet, El Salvador

20   Liberating God,
            free us from wrong-headed religion and ritual,
            from self-indulgence and self-deceit,
            that we may share the joy of your freedom
            in unbinding those who live in darkness
            and in the shadow of death.

Joy Tetley, England

21   Lord, we do not always find it easy to recognize your coming to us. Often our spirits are downcast and we, who looked for so much in Christ, are frankly disappointed. Will you reveal yourself to us? Open our eyes to undiscovered secrets of your Word. Meet us in the breaking of bread. Set our heavy hearts on fire with love for you and send us on our way rejoicing. For your name's sake.

Ian D Bunting, England

Food to pilgrims given,   22
strength upon the way;
bread come down from heaven –
Christ is ours today!
Feed us now, O Lord, with this holy food –
let your kingdom come, O Lord, let your kingdom come;
let your kingdom come, O Lord, let your kingdom come.

Streams of grace are flowing –
life from death for me;
truth and goodness growing
for eternity.
Cleanse my soul, O Lord, with your precious blood –
let your will be done, O Lord, let your will be done;
let your will be done, O Lord, let your will be done.

I receive your blessing –
Jesus, king divine;
all your love confessing
in this bread and wine.
Send me out, O Lord, holy, pure and good,
till the world is won, O Lord, till the world is won;
till the world is won, O Lord, till the world is won.

Geonyong Lee, Korea

23 Far beyond our mind's grasp and our tongue's declaring,
in a holy mystery, quietly, truly you are here;
lifted once on Calvary, sin and weakness bearing,
O Lord, how wonderful you call us to draw near!

None of us is worthy to receive your essence
in this meal together; yet this gift is yours by choice;
death can never snatch us from your holy presence.
Your promise is for life; we only can rejoice.

So our hearts are lifted to the realms above us,
nourished and united by the precious bread and wine:
here what sweet contentment, knowing that you love us!
We thank you for this feast, this fellowship divine.

Soon you bid us scatter – share what we inherit –
from this house of blessing where we taste your peace
    and grace.
May our lives be altars glowing with your Spirit
to light the lamps of those who also seek your face.

Francisco F Feliciano, Philippines

BAPTISM AND EUCHARIST

Lord, we stand awed   24
in the presence of your evangelist:
this tiny baby thing who dares
to be your child!

Not one word can she speak,
this your little messenger;
yet in the silence she declares
the living Word!

She has no prior faith
and brings no creed or prayer,
but from this font she bears
the faith of Christ!

She offers now no promises
nor deeds of righteousness,
but here receives and shares
the righteousness of God!

Helpless, she comes today,
carried in the arms of others,
yet in her helplessness she wears
your massive strength!

Lord, this is the greatest thing:
here a child has Brother, Friend,
and a Father who cares
world without end!

Bruce D Prewer, Australia

25   Thank you, Father, for your free gift of fire.
Because it is through fire that you draw near to us every day.
It is with fire that you constantly bless us.
Our Father, bless this fire today.
With your power enter into it.
Make this fire a worthy thing.
A thing that carries your blessing.
Let it become a reminder of your love.
A reminder of life without end.
Make the life of these people to be baptized like this fire.
A thing that shines for the sake of people.
A thing that shines for your sake.
Father, heed this sweet-smelling smoke.
Make their life also sweet smelling.
A thing sweet smelling that rises to God.
A holy thing.
A thing fitting for you.

Masai people, Tanzania

26   May this Eucharist,
conquering doubt and fear,
be for everyone
a sign of your passage in our lives,
as we wait for you
in order to live
today.

Pierre Talec, France

What a long road has been travelled 27
since the day the risen Christ
revealed himself
to the disciples from Emmaus!

Yet it is the same road
we walk again today:
Christ is still speaking,
still celebrating the Eucharist.

May his words
and the breaking of the bread,
shared down through the centuries,
renew in us
the fidelity of love
amid the drab realities of life!

Pierre Talec, France

We thank you, gracious God, 28
that we are the guests at your table.
As we have been fed by your gifts of life,
so we will share with the world
all that you give to us in love.

Dorothy McRae-McMahon, Australia

29

Am I mistaken, Lord,
is it a temptation to think
You increasingly urge me
to go forth and proclaim
the need and urgency
of passing
from the Blessed Sacrament
to your other presence,
just as real,
in the Eucharist of the poor?
Theologians will argue,
a thousand distinctions be advanced . . .
But woe to him who feeds on you
and later has no eyes to see you,
to discern you
foraging for food among the garbage,
being evicted every other minute,
living in sub-human conditions
under the sign
of utter insecurity!

Dom Helder Camara, Brazil

O Risen Christ, who made yourself known to the disciples in the   30
breaking of the bread at Emmaus; the bread we break at this table
is a sign of the brokenness of all the world; through our sharing in
the Bread of Life in our many Christian communions, open our
eyes and hands to the needs of all people. Let our hearts burn to
share your gifts and help us to go forth with one another with
Bread: Bread of Hope, Bread of Life, Bread of Peace.

Prayer used at the 6th Assembly of the World Council of Churches, Vancouver

O God our Father, I thank you for giving me health and strength   31
to come to this Holy Communion service. I pray for the strength-
ening and refreshing of my soul by the Body and Blood of Christ,
as my body would be by bread and wine.

Help me to follow the example of your dear Son, by trying to
help others at all times. Show me the opportunities as they present
themselves and give me the courage to act upon them, through
Jesus Christ, our Lord.

Margaret Pollock, Ireland

32   My God, I need to have signs of your grace.
Serve me your sacraments,
the first fruits of your Kingdom.

I thirst for smiles,
   for sweet odours,
   for soft words,
   for firm gestures,
   for truth and goodness,
   and for triumphs
   (no matter how small)
   of justice.

You know, O God, how hard it is to survive captivity
without any hope of the Holy City.
Sing to us, God, the songs of the promised land.
Serve us your manna in the desert.

Let there be, in some place,
a community of men, women, elderly, children, and
   new-born babies
   as a first fruit,
   as our appetiser,
   and our embrace of the future.

Rubem A Alves, Brazil

CREEDS

I believe in one world, full of riches meant for   33
   everyone to enjoy;
I believe in one race, the family of mankind, learning
   how to live together by the hard way of self-sacrifice.
I believe in one life, exciting and positive;
   which enjoys all the beauty, integrity and science;
   uses the discipline of work to enrich society;
   harmonizes with the life of Jesus,
   and develops into a total joy.
I believe in one morality: love –
   the holiness of sharing the sorrow and joys
   of others;
   bringing together people as true friends;
   working to rid the world of the root causes of poverty
   and injustice, ignorance and fear;
love, the test of all my thoughts and motives;
love, guiding me, controlling me, assuring me of
   God's forgiveness;
   and giving me confidence under his Spirit's control.
I believe in Jesus, and the Bible's evidence about him;
   whose life, death and resurrection prove God's
   lasting love for the world;
   who combines in himself, life, love, truth,
   humanity, reality
   and God;
   who saves, guides, and unites all people who
   follow his way.
I believe in the purpose of God,
   to unite in Christ everything, spiritual or secular,
   to renew society, individuals and nations,
   and to guide all governments under his fatherly
   direction.

Indian National Industrial Mission

34   I believe, Lord,
that everything good in the world
comes from you.
I believe in your great love for all people.
I believe that, because you preached love,
freedom and justice,
you were humiliated,
tortured and killed.

I believe that you continue
to suffer in our people . . .
I believe that you call me
to defend your cause,
but I also believe that you accompany me
in the task of transforming this world
into a different one
where there is no suffering or weeping;
a world where there is a gigantic table
set with free food
where everyone is welcome.

I believe that you accompany us
in waiting for the dawning of a new day.
I believe that you will give us strength
so that death does not find us
without having done enough,
and that you will rise
in those who have died seeking a different world.

A peasant woman, El Salvador

CHRISTMAS

Lord Jesus, 35
you have come to live among us.
What do you think of us now?
Are you sorry you came?

Do not go away;
but be patient with us,
for you are one of us –
the one who saves.
Flesh of our flesh,
save our joy!

Pierre Talec, France

O sweet child of Bethlehem, grant that we may share with all our 36
hearts in this profound mystery of Christmas. Put into the hearts of
men this peace for which they sometimes seek so desperately and
which you alone can give them. Help them to know one another
better, and to live as children of the same Father.

Reveal to them also your beauty, holiness and purity. Awaken in
their hearts love and gratitude for your infinite goodness. Join them
all together in your love. And give us your heavenly peace.

Pope John XXIII

37   Jesus, many people rejoice because they have sought you
           and found you;
       but I rejoice because you have sought and found me.

       The shepherds of Bethlehem, to whom the angels appeared,
           were full of joy;
       they heard the message and saw the glory.
       But I am more joyful than the shepherds,
       because I have heard the Gospel from your own lips,
       and not from angels.
       You said to me: 'Come to me, and I will make your
           burden light.'
       That is why I am more joyful than the shepherds of
           Bethlehem.

       The wise men from the East saw the star and were happy;
       they searched you out and brought you presents.
       But I am happier than those wise men,
       because it is you who searched me out;
       you have brought me the richest present in the world,
           my salvation.
       That is why I am happier than the wise men from the East.

       Mary is blessed:
       as a baby, you dwelt forty weeks in her womb.
       But I am more blessed than Mary,
       because, all through my life
       you have dwelt in my heart, risen Christ.
       That is why I am more blessed than Mary, your Mother.

Simeon the prophet rejoiced as he sang,
'My eyes have seen your salvation.'
I have not seen you, but I have believed in you.
And since you called those happy who believe without seeing,
I have reached the peaks of contentment.

Johnson Gnanabaranam, India

Dear God, we will be very busy again this Christmastime, and we   38
know that we will be tempted to forget the true meaning of this
festival. Please help us to conquer these temptations, so that we may
share with our families the true joy of our Saviour's birth. Lord, we
have sung our Christmas carols and heard the Nativity story so
many times before; help us, in our acts of worship, to recapture the
wonder of this glad season. Please make each heart a manger and
each home a Bethlehem. We pray this in the name of Jesus Christ,
our Saviour.

Edith Williams, Wales

39

Lord Jesus,
for eternities now,
heaven and earth,
like fond grandparents,
have thrilled at the sight
of the children's children
ever bringing forth children . . .

And now,
amid the starlit night,
comes the incomparable Child,
the smile of God
and tenderness toward mankind.

We beg you, Lord,
revive in us
the joy of your joy
for ever and ever.

Pierre Talec, France

Jesus, 40
    how clearly we see you at Christmas-time,
    cradled by Mary,
    protected by Joseph,
    worshipped by shepherds,
    honored by kings,
    enshrined on the altar,
    and loved by the world.

But, oh Lord,
    help us look for you, too,
    among the taxes of life,
    and the wanderings of rootless travellers.
    In the world's smelly stables,
    and in makeshift mangers.
    In sweat-like drops of blood
    and rough-hewn crosses, humanly fashioned.
    Help us look, Lord –
    and help us find!

Not only at Christmas,
    but throughout a New Year that it might become indeed
    'the year of our Lord'.

Mary Sue H Rosenberger, United States

41   Here is Good News . . .
The very Son of God became a human being,
to live among us.
The manner of his coming
surprised us . . .

We did not recognize his coming;
only some shepherds
and three mystics came from another country.
But we,
Jews, Europeans, Africans,
peoples of the world,
were not there.

He offended us.
We did not see the sign
to us and to all peoples:
the sign of an ordinary baby,
   wrapped in Jewish swaddling bands;
the sign of an African baby,
   born on banana leaves.
It was too insignificant!
But here is the Gospel . . .
That the Son of God has come *down* to us,
the Word of God made flesh,
alive in the world,
full of grace and truth.

Maureen Edwards, Kenya

Jesus, as a baby you were a refugee, as a man, you had no place to 42
lay your head. Make us aware of the homeless on our streets and of
families without adequate shelter. Give us wisdom to deal with the
causes of these problems, that all may work together for better living
conditions.

Women's World Day of Prayer, 1988

God of heaven, 43
you came to earth to claim your own,
and your own received you not.
Claim us and hold us, we pray,
in our flesh and to all eternity.

Joy Tetley, England

O God, who by a star guided the wise men to the worship of your 44
Son: we pray you to lead to yourself the wise and the great of every
land, that unto you every knee may bow, and every thought be
brought into captivity; through Jesus Christ our Lord.

Epiphany collect from the Church of South India, adapted

45   O God, our Father, Creator of the universe, whose Son, Jesus Christ, came to our world, pour your Holy Spirit upon your Church, that all the people of our world, being led through the knowledge of your truth to worship you, may offer the gold of intellect, the frankincense of devotion and the myrrh of discipline to him who is with you and the Holy Spirit who liveth and reigneth for ever one God, world without end.

Church of Ceylon (Sri Lanka)

EASTER

THE CROSS

Jesus, each of us is both the thief who blasphemes   46
and the one who believes.
I have faith, Lord, help my lack of faith.
I am nailed to death, there is nothing I can do
but cry out: 'Jesus, remember me
when you come with your kingdom.'

Jesus, I know nothing, I understand nothing
in this horrific world.
But you, you come to me, with open arms,
with open heart,
and your presence alone is my paradise.
Ah, remember me
when you come with your kingdom.

Glory and praise to you, you who welcome
not the healthy but the sick,
you whose unexpected friend is a criminal
cut off by the justice of men.
Already you are going down to hell and setting free
those who cry out to you:
'Remember us, Lord,
when you come with your kingdom.'

Ecumenical Patriarch Bartholomew of the Orthodox Church

47   Pieces of wood,
broken and burnt,
stained with blood of family,
derelict in the smouldering heap.
The smell of death
in dusty roads,
sounds of weeping,
darkness and gloom.

Pieces of wood
pierce the wounded side,
lightning and thunder,
shots of gunfire,
rending cries of
mothers and daughters
in the sleepless houses
waiting for the first light.

My God, my God, why have you abandoned us?
why have you forgotten us,
forsaken us?

Cry rage and revenge,
slaughter and destruction.
How long will this be,
terror in the faces of children,
hatred and fear,
over a wilderness of shacks,
the other side of the city wall,
longing for peace?

My God, my God, why have you abandoned us?
why have you forgotten us,
forsaken us?

Come,
let us carry these pieces of wood,
once part of the same ancient tree
used to build houses, proud and sturdy,
now charred ruins of dwelling places,
scattered and aloof.

Bind piece with piece
to build one cross.

Cross of Bhambayi,
shelter me,
hide me from the
pain and agony,
as the blood,
like justice,
flows from the cross.

From the soil
sprouts a new year of freedom and healing
for captives
maimed in body and
maimed in hope.

Sacred mystery
on this holy ground,
tree of redemption,
the flowering tree which withers
and blossoms again
from Eden to Calvary
to Easter . . .
in Bhambayi . . .

Devarakshanam Betty Govinden, Kwa-Zulu Natal, South Africa
(Bhambayi is a violence-ravaged place just outside the city of Durban.)

48 O Lord Jesus, forgive me for the times I have racked you on the cross of God's purpose and my rebellion. Let me gaze at that cross and recognize what my wilfulness has done. So join my grief with your passion, Lord; that with your whole creation I may be redeemed.

Ruth Etchells, England

49   God of all goodness,
        by the hell and victory of the cross
        embolden us to come to you
        with our loud cries and tears,
        to receive mercy and help
        in time of need.

Joy Tetley, England

50 Great God, our Father: as we call to mind the scene of Christ's suffering in Gethsemane, our hearts are filled with penitence and shame that we foolishly waste our time in idleness and that we make no progress in the Christian life from day to day... We are ashamed that war and lust flourish and grow more rampant every day. Forgive us for our cruel indifference to the cross, and pardon us that, like the bystanders of old, we merely stand and gaze in idle curiosity upon the piteous scene. O teach us, we beseech thee, the good news of thy forgiveness. Cause humanity, degenerate as it is, to live anew, and hasten the day when the whole world shall be born again.

Toyohiko Kagawa, Japan

FROM GOOD FRIDAY TO EASTER DAY

Lord Jesus, 51
you alone can reveal to us
the riches of God's solitude
in the communion of persons.

Alone in the desert
and alone in Gethsemane,
alone on your cross,
between men who were alone on theirs,
you assumed everyone's solitude
within yourself
so that everyone might commune
with God.

O God of encounters,
may each of us
in his desert
detect a sign of your presence.
With you,
may each of us be
for his brothers
a travelling companion
in the fellowship of the Father
and the Spirit.

Lord Jesus,
by taking part
in your death and resurrection,
we pass from solitude to communion.

Pierre Talec, France

52

Nailed to a cross because you would not
compromise on your convictions.
Nailed to a cross because you would not
bow down before insolent might.
My Saviour, you were laughed at,
derided, bullied, and spat upon
but with unbroken spirit,
Liberator God, you died.

Many young lives are sacrificed
because they will not bend;
many young people in prison
for following your lead.
Daily, you are crucified,
my Saviour, you are sacrificed
in prison cells and torture rooms
of cruel and ruthless powers.

The promise of resurrection,
the power of hope it holds,
and the vision of a just new order
you proclaimed that first Easter morning.
Therefore, dear Saviour, we can affirm
that although bodies are mutilated and broken,
the spirit refuses submission.
Your voice will never be silenced,
Great Liberating God.

Aruna Gnanadason, India

O Christ, as we walk through the land that you loved, in the country   53
where you lived and taught, grant us the grace and wisdom to see
clearly and understand deeply that all you suffered was for the sake
of redeeming humanity. Through your life, death, and resurrection,
you have made it possible for us to have life, and have it more
abundantly.

O Christ, as we follow you down the Road to Calvary,
Guide us to become active participants, not curious bystanders.
O Christ, as we stand with the mourners at the Cross,
Give us the love that can forgive those who trespass against us.
O Christ, as we witness the new life given to us through your
    Resurrection,
Empower us with faith to act and spread the Good News.

Palestinian women of Jerusalem

THE RESURRECTION

54   In the light of Easter dawn,
            while disciples in whispers
            passed their despair one to another,
        you arose at the call of the Father,
        bringing light and immortality to light,
            warming hearts with inextinguishable joy,
            and rehabilitating doubters and deniers
        with a love that overpowers the gates of hell.

        Jesus, the Word made flesh,
            Jesus, friend of sinners,
        Reconciler of the whole universe,
            the resurrection and the life:
        Heaven and earth are full of your glory!
        Our allegiance and gratitude are yours for ever!

Bruce D Prewer, Australia

55   God of new beginnings,
        free us from the fear of change.
        May our experience of Easter
        so change our lives
        that they express your boundless love.

Joy Tetley, England

56 O Christ, you are united to every human being without exception.
    Still more, risen from the dead, you come to heal the secret wound
    of our soul. And for each of us there opens the gates of an infinite
    goodness of heart. Through such love, little by little our hearts are
    changed.

Brother Roger of Taizé, France

When the broken come to wholeness,
when the wounded come to healing,
when the frightened come to trusting,

the stone has been rolled away.

When the lonely find friendship,
when the hurt find new loving,
when the worried find peace,

the stone has been rolled away.

When we share instead of taking,
when we stroke instead of striking,
when we join around the table,

the stone has been rolled away.

The stone has been rolled away!
In you, Christ Jesus,
love breaks through hatred,
hope breaks through despair,
life breaks through death.
Hallelujah, Christ is risen!

Francis Brienen, United Kingdom

58   Christ Jesus is here –
      here,
      as on the first day;
      here among us eternally,
      as on Easter morning;
      here with us for ever
      as fully as on the first day;
      here in our midst
      through all the days of his eternity:
      for he is risen!
      Alleluia!

Pierre Talec, France

59 O Lord God, our Father. You are the light that can never be put out; and now you give us a light that shall drive away all darkness. You are love without coldness, and you have given us such warmth in our hearts that we can love all when we meet. You are the life that defies death, and you have opened for us the way that leads to eternal life.

  None of us is a great Christian; we are all humble and ordinary. But your grace is enough for us. Arouse in us that small degree of joy and thankfulness of which we are capable, to the timid faith which we can muster, to the cautious obedience which we cannot refuse, and thus to the wholeness of life which you have prepared for all of us through the death and resurrection of your Son. Do not allow any of us to remain apathetic or indifferent to the wondrous glory of Easter, but let the light of our risen Lord reach every corner of our dull hearts.

Karl Barth, Switzerland

Lord,
you left the grave,
walked in the garden,
revealed yourself to Mary,
came to your disciples.

60

Death could not hold you,
evil was overcome,
the prince of darkness defeated;
the Father had acted
through his eternal Son.

Your disciples seeing you,
believed, understood and obeyed.
You gave them your Spirit,
the Holy One,
and they made you known.

Generation upon generation
know you never change.
Your love still reaches out.
Your crucifixion and resurrection
still restore our inheritance.

Your light pierces our darkness,
your truth makes us whole,
your love bursts into our lives,
your joy fills our needy souls,
because we know you are alive.

Jesus, Lord,
you are alive!
You are alive!

Pamela Wilding, Kenya

61

O Risen Christ, you go down
to the lowest depths
of our human condition,
and you burden yourself
with what burdens us.
Still more, you even go
to visit those who have died
without being able to know you.

And even when within us
we can hear no refrain
of your presence,
you are there.
Through your Holy Spirit
you remain with us.

Brother Roger of Taizé, France

PENTECOST

Wind of God, blow far from us   62
all dark despair,
all deep distress,
all groundless fears,
all sinful desires,
all Satan's snares,
all false values,
all selfish wishes,
all wasteful worries.

Blow into us
your holy presence,
your living love,
your healing touch,
your splendid courage,
your mighty strength,
your perfect peace,
your caring concern,
your divine grace,
your boundless joy.

Wind of God,
blow strong,
    blow fresh,
        blow now.

Pamela Wilding, Kenya

63   Spirit of God, active in creation:
Spirit of love,
Spirit of Jesus, one with our Saviour:
Spirit of love,
Spirit of life, present in the Church:
Spirit of love.

We rejoice in your presence
around us and in us,
through the precious Gospel of Christ,
like wind on our faces
and breath in our lungs:
Presence of joy.

We rejoice in your power
to give new birth and new life,
like fire, warmth and radiance,
like life in dormant daffodils
bursting forth in spring:
Presence of hope.

We rejoice in your accepting us,
ceaselessly seeking us,
freely treasuring us,
with love older than mountains
or the distant stars,
new every morning:
Presence of grace.

Creator Spirit:
Spirit of love,
Life-giving Spirit:
Spirit of love,
Nurturing Spirit:
Spirit of love,

We bless you for your mercy,
love you and adore you.
Blessed be your name
of love for ever and ever.

Bruce D Prewer, Australia

O surging Spirit, mighty wind of God, blow through my heart   64
today. Let me not fear your energy and force, but welcome it in my
life. Let it disperse all those accretions, those patterns of life and
worship I have come to rely on and take pleasure in for their own
sake rather than as ways to you. Disturb my complacencies, Lord,
the things I cling to for security in place of clinging to you. And in
their place give me the wonder of your fire, of God's holy flames
above my head and in my heart.

O gentle Spirit, breathing on the face of the waters in those
depths of my heart still unformed and in darkness; in that deepest
part of me where there is still chaos, shape your order and harmony,
bring forth your design in new life.

O creator Spirit, make me a channel of your creative life in the
world. Empower me to help others towards new life, and enable me
to reject all that within me is destructive or malign or repressive. Let
me rejoice selflessly in your creative work in others, glorying in the
wonders of God in other people's lives. And bond us together in the
life and calling of the Church, whose day of birth we celebrate
today. Keep us aflame with your new life for the world. In the love
and power of the triune God, Father, Son and Holy Spirit.

Ruth Etchells, England

65 Like the wind swaying through mountain trees,
   or surging through thickets of wattle,
so, Lord, is your presence with us;
   your power thrusts through our lives.
You sweep away our petty worries
   and shake us free from fears.
At your pressure we move and sway together,
   as if we were of one mind.

Sometimes you are as strong as winter storms,
   at others as soft as the rustling of ferns.
We are taught to bend and not be broken,
   to be flexible without shifting ground.
You test the strength of our feet
   and whatever proves shallow is uprooted.

On calm days we rest content,
   glad to watch each other in stillness;
enjoying quietness because we know
   you are still with us.

Bruce D Prewer, Australia

66 Breath of Christ's loving, Holy Spirit, in the depths of our soul you
set faith. It is like a burst of trusting repeated countless times in the
course of our life. It can only be a simple act of trust, so simple that
all can welcome it.

Brother Roger of Taizé, France

Holy Spirit of God, all-powerful as the wind you came to the 67
Church on the Day of Pentecost to quicken its life and empower
its witness. Come to us now as the Wind of Heaven and breathe
new life into our souls; and revive your work among us, that God
in all things may be glorified, through Jesus Christ our Lord.

Church of England

O God our heavenly Father, as we light this candle and watch the 68
flame grow, kindle within us afresh the flame of your Holy Spirit. Let
us so glow with your love that others may see you in us and want
to know you; in our homes, our Church, our parish, our diocese.
Bless those who light candles each day as a token of witness to the
light of your power and glory; and to the coming of your kingdom
on earth. This we ask in the name of Jesus.

Women of St Asaph diocese, Wales

Spirit of joy, with us always, 69
through you, Christ lives in us, and we in Christ.
Forgive us when we forget you
and when we fail to live in your joy.

Spirit of love, with us always.
You bind us in love to yourself
and to those around us.
Forgive us when we hurt those we love
and when we turn away
from the love of our friends.

The people of Pitt Street Uniting Church, Sydney, Australia

70

Touch me, God's Spirit eternal,
touch me, resplendent Light;
give my life new meaning,
show me the true and right.

Touch me, God's Spirit, and soothe me
deep in my restless soul;
give me trust in Jesus,
heal me and make me whole.

Spirit of God, give me courage,
banish my doubts and fears;
show me my vocation
through all my days and years.

Spirit of God, brightly shining,
open my eyes to see
those who need my friendship –
join us in unity.

Touch me, God's Spirit eternal,
teach me to thank and praise;
by your grace be near me,
guide me in all my ways.

Pia Perhïo, Finland

Eternal father, you sent your Son to bring the Good News of your   71
forgiving love to us sinners. Your Son in turn sent the Holy Spirit
to continue his mission on earth through the Church. Quicken us,
we pray, by the same Spirit that we shall not rest until all people are
reached with your Gospel, through Jesus Christ our Lord.

Naftali Okello Siwa, Kenya

We present ourselves before you in adoration of your holy majesty,   72
conscious of our own indignity, but also of the action of your grace
shown in the many gifts which you never cease to give us, gifts both
of body and of spirit. We thank you especially that, on this Sunday
and this festival, we remember that your well beloved Son, our Lord
Jesus Christ, did not leave us orphans when he returned to your
presence. He wanted, until he returns in glory, to remain close to
us through the Holy Spirit, whose reviving strength teaches and
comforts us.

Grant us to recognise this great benefit, and to praise you for it.
Help us, whenever your word is preached and understood in this
place and wherever your people gather, to call on your name.
Sanctify and bless the celebration of the holy eucharist in which we
are about to share. Let your light illumine us. Let your peace be
among us.

Karl Barth, Switzerland

73   Holy Spirit of God,
           you came on the Day of Pentecost,
           to change the lives of the disciples,
           who had hidden themselves in the Upper Room
               for fear of the Jews.

Come amongst us, we pray you,
       to transform our lives.
Make Jesus real to us,
       reassuring us and strengthening our faith in him.

Set us apart for the service of Jesus,
       not taking us out of the world,
       but sending us into it,
       to proclaim boldly the good news of his saving love.

Spirit of Life, come into our lives
       and make them alive with the Life of Jesus,
       our Living Saviour.

For his name's sake.

William N Richards and James Richardson, Kenya

74   Our experience is precisely that weakness is our strength, that the wind of the Spirit, within and outside the boundaries of the churches, has less to blow down when our structures are of mud and straw rather than concrete! Perhaps we should be thankful for our fragility; it is just that that keeps us on our toes.

Members of a Christian ashram, India

Almighty God, our heavenly Father, the privilege is ours to be 75
called to share in the loving, healing and reconciling mission of
your Son Jesus Christ our Lord in this age and wherever we are.
Since without you we can do no good thing:

may your Spirit make us wise;
may your Spirit guide us;
may your Spirit renew us;
may your Spirit strengthen us
so that we will be:

strong in faith;
discerning in proclamation;
courageous in witness;
persistent in good deeds.

This we ask through the same Jesus Christ our Lord.

Church of the West Indies

Holy Spirit, Spirit of the Living God, 76
you breathe in us
on all that is inadequate and fragile.

You make living water spring even
from our hurts themselves. And
through you, the valley of tears
becomes a place of wellsprings.

So, in an inner life
with neither beginning nor end,
your continual presence
makes new freshness break through.

Brother Roger of Taizé, France

GIVING THANKS

Almighty God, creator of earth and all that is in it, you are the God   77
of our ancestors – those living on earth and those in the spiritual
world. We praise and honour you for your love and care, for all the
blessings of life and for your protection. It is you who clothes the
world every season and cares for every living creature. Help us to
treat all sacred places with honour and reverence.

We have not forgotten your anger towards us when you closed
down the sky and did not give us enough rains for many years. We
agree that we went astray and left your ways. We may have wronged
those in the spiritual world and yourself. But in the end you had
mercy on us and opened up the sky. We are only human beings who
are prone to making mistakes unknowingly; forgive us.

But life is still very hard for us, God our creator. Medical expenses
and education for our children are very expensive. We have lost
hope of any change for the better. We ask you to save us from this
difficult situation. We are perishing from the scourge of AIDS. Jobs
are very difficult to come by. The price of basic commodities goes
up every day. We are struggling to survive. Help us as we continue
the struggle.

Claudius M Matsikiti, Zimbabwe

78 Lord of all creation, you speak to us through your creatures of your beauty and grace and humour and the loveliness of your form. So often, Lord, we take your gifts for granted, so often we are blind, so often we are brutal, so often we try to prove our superiority or make a profit out of your creatures. In their silence and suffering you rebuke us and sometimes by riding on a donkey you show us their beauty. Lord, this day let me not miss the loveliness of flowers or reject the loveliness of your animals, for if I do that, I fear I may miss you altogether.

Subir Biswas, India

79 Almighty God, your word of creation caused the water to be filled with many kinds of living beings and the air to be filled with birds. With those who live in this world's small islands we rejoice in the richness of your creation, and we pray for your wisdom for all who live on this earth, that we may wisely manage and not destroy what you have made for us and for our descendants. In Jesus' name we pray.

Unknown, Samoa

FOOD FOR THE WORLD

May our yams,   80
which we are going to plant in the earth this year,
be good.
May children be born.
May we have enough to eat.
Let us live.
If anyone should cast a spell over anyone else,
let that one die.
Let peace reign among us.

Yakö people, Nigeria

Almighty God, Lord of heaven and earth, we humbly pray that your   81
gracious care may give and preserve the seeds which we plant in
our farms that they may bring forth fruit in good measure; that we
who constantly receive from your goodness may always give thanks
to you, the giver of all good things; through Jesus Christ, your Son
our Lord.

Unknown, Cameroon

82

Lord,
isn't your creation wasteful?
Fruits never equal
the seedlings' abundance.
Springs scatter water.
The sun gives out
enormous light.
May your bounty teach me
greatness of heart.
May your magnificence
stop me being mean.
Seeing you a prodigal
and open-handed giver,
let me give unstintingly . . .
like God's own.

Dom Helder Camara, Brazil

83

God, food of the poor;
Christ, our bread,
give us a taste of the tender bread
from your creation's table;
bread newly taken
from your heart's oven,
food that comforts and nourishes us.
A fraternal loaf that makes us human;
joined hand in hand,
working and sharing.
A warm loaf that makes us a family;
sacrament of your body,
your wounded people.

Workers in community soup kitchens, Lima, Peru

Heavenly Father, 84
  you have created the countryside:
  its fields and forests,
  hills and rivers,
  birds and animals
  and fresh, healthy air to breathe.
We thank you for all this goodness and beauty.

Help those for whom rural life is hard and difficult:
  those who must travel far to collect firewood
  and bring their water from distant streams:
  all who live in poor conditions.

Bless the efforts being made to improve conditions
  in rural areas,
  so that the people who work to feed this nation,
  may themselves enjoy a higher standard of living.

William N Richards and James Richardson, Kenya

O Spirit, grant us a calm lake, little wind, little rain, so that the 85
canoes may proceed well, so that they may proceed speedily.

Fishermen's prayer, Tanzania

THE WORLD WE LIVE IN

86   O Lord, we are guilty of always demanding more and more material possessions. We encourage industry and science to produce more and more goods to satisfy our every need. Our houses are full of things we do not need. Unnecessary packaging pollutes our environment. We ask for your forgiveness. Help us to show how we can use material things in a responsible way. Open our eyes that we may learn to live wisely with all your creation.

Women's World Day of Prayer, 1992,
written by women from Austria, Germany and Switzerland

87   Father God,
     just as children spoil their presents,
     so we abuse your good gifts to us.

We dump rubbish in the rivers.
     We leave litter on the streets.
     Our beaches are contaminated with oil.
     The air is filled with fumes and smells.
     Noisy machines and radios destroy our peace.
     And so many of these things we allow in the name of progress.

Give us a greater respect for the world you entrust to us,
     so that by our greed and selfishness,
     we do not destroy or spoil,
     that which we could never have created for ourselves.

William N Richards and James Richardson, Kenya

Grandfather, 88
look at our brokenness.
We know that in all creation
only the human family
has strayed away from the sacred way.
We know that we are the ones
who are divided,
and we are the ones
who must come back together
to walk in the sacred way.
Grandfather, sacred one,
teach us love, compassion and honour
that we may heal the earth
and heal each other.

The Ojibway nation of Canada

Enjoy the earth gently, 89
enjoy the earth gently,
for if the earth is spoiled,
it cannot be repaired.
Enjoy the earth gently.

Yoruba people, Nigeria

THE CHURCH

THE CHURCH'S LIFE

God of surprises,   90
when I think you are not present in my life,
you reveal yourself in the love of friends and family
and nurture me in your never-ending affection.

God of surprises,
when we think you are not present in our community,
you labour to make us of one heart
and cause us to share gladly and generously.

God of surprises,
when people think you are not present in our world,
you bring hope out of despair
and create growth out of difficulty.

God of surprises,
you are ever with us.

When the days go by and our vision fades,
keep surprising us.
When our hope dims and our patience wears thin,
keep coming to us.
Teach us to keep our lamps lit
and to be prepared,
that we may see your loving presence among us.

Francis Brienen, United Kingdom

91 Lord, make us realize that our Christianity is like a rice field, that when it is newly planted, the paddies are prominent; but as the plants take root and grow taller, these dividing paddies gradually vanish, and soon there appears only one vast continuous field. So give us roots of love and make us grow in Christian fellowship and service, so that thy will be done in our lives, through our Saviour, thy Son, Jesus Christ.

Philippines

92 Forgive us, Lord, when sometimes we think and act as if only *we* have the devotion to you and to your children. We need the strength of each other to continue to serve all your creatures. Thank you for giving us companions on the way.

Subir Biswas, India

93
O God who travels with us in the shadows,
you know who we are.
We long for life which is full and free.
We long to know the truth
and we want to leave behind us
all the things which hold us back.

We want to move forward in faith
but the way seems so dangerous
and we stand in helpless fear
before the hiddenness in our past
and in our future.

The people of Pitt Street Uniting Church, Sydney, Australia

O Lord: 94

In a world where many are lonely,
we thank you for our friendships.

In a world where many are captive,
we thank you for our freedom.

In a world where many are hungry,
we thank you for your provision.

We pray that you will:
enlarge our sympathy,
deepen our compassion,
and give us grateful hearts.

In Christ's name.

Terry Waite, England

We are very glad you are with us, O God.   95
There are times when it feels
as though there might be no one else.
Sometimes it seems as though you too have left us alone.
But here, together, we claim your company in faith
and ask you to travel with us through this day and our lives.

Dorothy McRae-McMahon, Australia

96 O Lord, Jesus Christ, Son of God, deliver us from deception of the imminent, loathsome and cunning Antichrist and from all his evil designs.

Protect all of us, and all our fellow Christians from his insidious traps, and shelter us within the hidden desert of your salvation.

Do not let us, O Lord, succumb to the fear of the devil, rather than abide in the fear of God, and let us not abandon you and your holy Church.

Better grant us, O Lord, to suffer and die for your holy name and the Orthodox Faith, rather than to renounce you; spare us from the Antichrist's seal of damnation and from worship of him.

Give us tears day and night, O Lord, to weep about our sins, and be merciful to us, O Lord, in the Day of Judgement.

Russian Orthodox believers in the old Soviet Union

97 O God, by your providence the blood of the martyrs is the seed of the Church: grant that we who remember before you the blessed martyrs of Uganda may, like them, be steadfast in our faith in Jesus Christ, in whom they gave obedience, even to death, and by their sacrifice brought forth a plentiful harvest.

Collect for the martyrs of Uganda

O Lord, whose holy saints and martyrs in all times and places have   98
endured affliction, suffering and tribulation, by the power of the
Holy Cross, the armour of salvation: so likewise, we pray, send your
Holy Spirit, the Comforter and Advocate of all Christians, to sustain these Churches in their martyrdom, witness and mission. The
world without provocation hates your Church, but you have taught
us not to despair. Therefore, you who are a God at hand and not a
God afar off, grant to these Christians the power to lift up their
hands, their eyes and their hearts to continue their living witness in
unity with the universal Church, to the glory of your most holy
name.

Unknown, Romania

THE CHURCH'S MINISTRY

99   God of illumination,
you call us beyond our imagining
to tasks beyond our powers.
Empower our service and enlighten our worship
that we may know and proclaim the light of the world.

Joy Tetley, England

100   Lord Jesus,
call out of our busy and competitive life
those whom you want to serve you as ministers
in your Church.
Save them from worldly ambition,
purify them of unworthy motives,
prepare them for a life of self-sacrifice,
fill them with a spirit of dedication to you,
and instruct them in your word and truth.

Send back those, whom you have called,
into the problems and opportunities of everyday life,
to be identified with those for whom you died,
as witnesses to your saving power
and as examples of the better life, which you
want us all to enjoy.

William N Richards and James Richardson, Kenya

This is my whole life, O Lord,   101
to know your word and teach it,
to know your word and live it.
Teach me, O Lord,
to proclaim what you teach and
to live how you live,
through Jesus Christ.

Bishop B A Kwashi, Nigeria

O God, Sustainer of all life and Creator of the universe, you set 102
aside men and women to be leaders, so help us to see things as they
are and not only as they affect ourselves. Grant that we may have a
wise and modest estimate of our own powers and live in full con-
tact with all things high, true and good. Teach us our failings and
our faults; give us courage to acknowledge them and by your grace
enable us to overcome them.

Lift us above the unstable currents of our self-will and establish
us on the rock of your purposes. Be to each of us the secret stay and
the inner guide of our lives. May your Spirit dwell in us more and
more, that your peace which exceeds all understanding may possess
our hearts and minds.

Lawrence Gandiya, Zimbabwe

Jesus, make our hearts ever gentler and more humble,   103
so that we may be present to those you have confided to
   our care,
and in this way make us instruments of your love
which gives life and joy and real freedom.

Jean Vanier, Canada

104   Let us pray for all those, throughout the world, who believe in
the Gospel:
that they may grow in grace and humanity.
Let us also pray for all Churches, that they may not lay up
treasures on earth or become monuments to a past age,
clinging to what is already dead and remote from people
of today,
but that they may be converted and receive the spirit of Jesus,
our Lord, who is the light and life, hope and peace of this
world, for ever and ever.

Huub Oosterhuis, Holland

105   O Lord, open my eyes
that I may see the need of others,
open my ears that I may hear their cries,
open my heart so that they need not be without succour.
Let me not be afraid to defend the weak
because of the anger of the strong,
nor afraid to defend the poor
because of the anger of the rich.
Show me where love and hope and faith are needed,
and use me to bring them to these places.
Open my eyes and ears that I may, this coming day,
be able to do some work of peace for you.

Alan Paton, South Africa

Heavenly Lord, we thank you that in your transcendence and hid- 106
denness you have made yourself known through revelation. Thank
you, too, for the scriptures which are the embodiment of your
dealings with our spiritual forefathers. We thank you that despite
the limitation and fallibility of human language, you have made it
possible for the divine revelation to be expressed in human language.

Inspire, we pray, those involved in translation and evangelism, that
guided by your Spirit they may accurately identify idioms, symbols
and other aspects of culture, that fully express your divine truth.
Lead them to consider avenues of communicating your message
through the words of our time, that nature and culture may join in
singing your eternal glory and praise, and through them your
Gospel may be published abroad.

Amos Ouma Okumu, Kenya

107   God the stranger, help us to welcome you
         to our land, our street, our home, our church.
         God the anonymous, help us to know you
         in lives that touch ours at a thousand points.
         God the helpless one, may we see you
         when you are cradled in a mother's arms.
         God the seed, the newborn, the beginning,
         help us to find our hope in you.

         We thank you, pioneering God,
         for the visionaries of faith
         who see more clearly
         and work more boldly
         because they have seen you
         in love, in suffering and in new life.

                        Bernard Thorogood, United Kingdom

108   Thank you, Lord, for doors long closed which by your grace are
      now opening in some countries. As we go forward, may we use
      prayer as a key to open new doors, to change systems that are
      unjust, to bring wholeness.

      We rejoice that as Lord of the universe, you allow humanity to
      unveil your creation beyond the earth. This unexpected door, which
      is slowly opening, leads us to marvel at your creation and to reflect
      on the importance of our part in the new life before us.

                        Women's World Day of Prayer, 1988

94

Our Heavenly Father, in the mighty name of our Lord Jesus Christ, 109
we want to thank you for the Church which is your own creation.
We want to thank you for the way you have enabled your servants,
by the power of the Holy Spirit, to propagate your Gospel throughout the world. We thank you for the zeal that you implanted in the
hearts of those early missionaries who brought the Good News to
Africa.

It is our prayer, Almighty God, that the power of the Holy Spirit
may work in the Church today, that the hearts of the people may
grow from strength to strength, that they may be able to withstand
the obstacles that come their way in their endeavour to make your
word reach all corners of the world. Revitalize your Church and let
your presence be with all who are called by your holy Name.

Help each of us to live according to your will so that your glory
may be found in your Church. Let everyone in the Church have
zeal to exalt your Name.

Francis M Kamau, Kenya

110   Most loving God,
you are the Shepherd God
who cares for us with an infinite compassion,
seeking to help even the smallest,
    weakest,
    and lowliest
    in your flock.

Grant to us, we pray,
the readiness to put ourselves
under your direction,
that in our weakness
we may have your divine support,
and in our strength
the wisdom to use our power
in ways that will not hurt others.

So shall we fulfil your purposes
declared in our Shepherd King,
Jesus Christ our Lord.

Bruce D Prewer, Australia

111 God our sovereign Lord, thank you for calling us and saving us to be your children. Our new life in you is a blessing for us. We pray for your strength; give us wisdom and understanding so that we may be led in your path. We look only for your signals and listen only to your voice, so that our deeds and words may reflect your divine calling. May our living be a model for the whole of creation.

Shaddrack Tanui Kipyegon, Kenya

MISSION

O Holy Spirit of God, help us to realise that there is no participa- 112
tion in Christ without participation in God's mission to the world.

Make us conscious of our calling as the body of Christ to fulfil that
mission.

Let us lay aside every weight and the sins which beset us and let us
run with patience the race that is set before us. 'And lo, I am with
you always even unto the end of the world.'

Women's World Day of Prayer, 1991,
written by women from Kenya

Jesus said, 'Peace be to you. Even as the Father sent me, so I send 113
you'. Almighty God, you sent your Son to bear the gift of fullness
of life to humanity. In perfect obedience he embraced your will and
drank the bitter cup; in perfect submission he walked the way of
suffering humanity; in perfect love he offered Himself on the altar
of Calvary that we might see light and life.

Through the same your Son, Jesus our Christ, your Church is
called and sent to be the mouth to speak for Jesus, the hands to do
his work. O God, you entrusted your message to the Church. Help
us to be obedient to this call; to seek your will. Help us to be sub-
missive, that all our strivings may be to accomplish the mission to
which you have called us. Help us to find and manifest that love
which is your benediction to us, that we may generate and sustain
in the place where we live that love which binds us together in
spite of our differences. May that love provide opportunities for
others to experience their own potential, and to know your presence
in them.

Ralston Smith, Jamaica

PROCLAIMING THE GOOD NEWS

114 Forgetting what lies behind and pressing on to the future, come
what may, we are resolved to reach every corner of our nation with
the Gospel of our Lord Jesus Christ.

You who are full of strength, call your people and put in their hearts
zeal for evangelism. Enable us as a church to train and equip those
you have called. Clothe them with your Spirit, empower us to proclaim Jesus King of all Kings.

The blood of the martyrs cannot allow us to rest when many of our
brothers and sisters know no salvation.

O God, you are our hiding place. Go before us and soften the hearts
of all these thy children whom the evil one has enslaved.

We put all our yearnings and cries before you with full assurance
that you will not throw us out. But that you rejoice greatly when
we fall on our knees and present our requests which you are ever
ready to grant, through Jesus Christ our Lord and Redeemer.

Church in Uganda

115 By the grace of God we are a pilgrim people, ever moving forward
and never settling down with the status quo. We bring our commitment to unity and mission, sharing with all the fullness of the
blessing of the Good News of Jesus Christ.
Holy God, fill us with the power of your Spirit that we may be your
witnesses to the ends of the earth.

Church of South India

Almighty God, you sent your only begotten Son Jesus Christ to die   116
for our sins. You sent your Holy Spirit to empower the disciples on
the Day of Pentecost. Send us out as your witnesses, filled with the
Holy Spirit, to proclaim the Gospel to all nations, carrying out the
great commission in obedience to the teaching of your Son, Jesus
Christ our Lord.

Church in Singapore

Almighty God, we thank you for having renewed your Church, at   117
various times and in various ways, by rekindling the fire of love for
you through the work of your Holy Spirit. Rekindle your love in
our hearts and renew us to fulfil the Great Commission which
your Son committed to us; so that, individually and collectively, as
members of your Church we may help many to know Jesus Christ
as their Lord and Saviour. Empower us by your Spirit to share, with
our neighbours and friends, our human stories in the context of
your divine story; through Jesus Christ our Lord.

Church in West Malaysia

118 Gracious Father, we humbly acknowledge our own sinfulness and waywardness.

We praise you that you freely forgive anyone who turns to you in repentance and faith.

Give each of us, we pray, such a fresh realisation of the wonder of the Gospel message that we may be constrained to share it gladly and graciously with others.

Grant that many people may enter into fullness of life in your Son, our Saviour, Jesus Christ.

Church of Ireland

119   Grant us, Lord God
the vision of your Kingdom,
forgiveness and new life,
and the stirring of your Spirit;
so that we may
share your vision,
proclaim your love,
and change this world,
in the Name of Christ.

Church in Australia

Pour your Light,
Holy Spirit of God,
into our hearts and minds.
Help us to know more clearly
and grasp more fully
the 'Good News' of Jesus.
And help us then
to know how to share it.
We ask this
through Jesus Christ who
with You and the Father
are One God.

120

Diocese of Zululand, South Africa

For a clearer vision of the work you have set before us and for a 121
better understanding of your Gospel,
  Lord, direct us.
For a deeper commitment in your service and a greater love for all
your children,
  Lord, direct us.
For a fresh understanding of the task before us and for a sense of
urgency in our proclamation,
  Lord, direct us.
For a greater respect and acceptance among Christians of different
traditions and for a common goal in evangelism,
  Lord, direct us.

Anglican Province of the Indian Ocean

122 Lord God of mission, grant, we beseech you, that the mission of Christ in the world may be fully accomplished through your Church. Inspire your servants to discover windows in different cultures through which the light of the Gospel may shine, that we may be able to share this precious treasure with others in language they fully understand. We pray for the work of Bible translation into the many human tongues, and for the work of writers articulating the same faith, that Christ may be fully incarnated into many cultures and your Church be established all over the world, through the risen Saviour Jesus Christ.

Naftali Okello Siwa, Kenya

123 Bless O Lord, those who hear your word and believe it. We pray for the people who are in remote areas, and live in fear of the world spirits, that they will know your power as Saviour of the world. Bring peace to our land and all parts of the world that are disturbed, so that the Gospel of Salvation may be preached to all mankind. In Jesus' Name we pray.

Episcopal Church of Sudan

LOVE IN ACTION

O God, our Father,   124
the fountain of love, power and justice,
the God who cares,
particularly for the least,
the most suffering and the poorest among us.

O God, Lord of creation,
grant us today your guidance and wisdom
so that we may see the human predicament for what it is.

Give us courage and obedience
so that we may follow you completely.
Help us, Lord, to bear witness
to the cross of your son, our Lord Jesus Christ,
who alone is the reason for hope,
and in whose name we pray.

Koson Srisang, Thailand

We need to communicate with each other across abysses of separa- 125
tion.

How can we let you enter into our lives, Lord, if we shut out our
sisters and brothers who share the earth with us?

From the bitterness and loneliness of keeping you and other
people outside our lives, save us, God. Nurture in us your love of
the whole of life that you have created.

Let us be faithful followers of your way of responsibility, unselfish
involvement in your people wherever they are found, and love.

Malcolm Boyd, United States

126   O God,
      enlarge my heart
      that it may be big enough to receive the greatness of your love.
      Stretch my heart
      that it may take into it all those who with me around the world
      believe in Jesus Christ.
      Stretch it
      that it may take into it all those who do not know him,
      but who are my responsibility because I know him.
      And stretch it
      that it may take in all those who are not lovely in my eyes,
      and whose hands I do not want to touch;
      through Jesus Christ, my saviour.

Prayer of an African Christian

127   Open my eyes that they may see
        the deepest needs of people.

        Move my hands that they may feed the hungry;
        touch my heart that it may bring warmth to the despairing;
        teach me the generosity that welcomes strangers;
        let me share my possessions to clothe the naked;
        give me the care that strengthens the sick;
        make me share in the quest to set the prisoner free.

        In sharing our anxieties and our love,
        our poverty and our prosperity,
        we partake of your divine presence.

Canaan Banana, Zimbabwe

O God, you took your Son   128
from our midst only to return
to us by way of your invisible Spirit.
Enable us, though we cannot see you
and even when we cannot feel your presence by way
of some mystical, supernatural experience,
to know that you dwell within us
and are here with us in our fellowship together.
May your Holy Spirit so abide in our hearts
and guide our activities
that we may walk in your paths for us
and accomplish those things
you would have us to do.
Thank you, Lord, for coming to us,
for the gift of your Spirit,
for redeeming us and commissioning us
to be your children and your servants,
your vessels and vehicles,
in the extending of your kingdom
in this world about us.

Leslie F Brandt, United States

129 Come to be our hope, Lord Jesus,
   come to set our people free;
from oppression come, release us,
   turn defeat to victory!
Come, release from every prison
   those who suffer in our land:
in your love we find the reason
   still to live and understand.

Come to build your new creation
   through the road of servanthood;
give new life to every nation,
   changing evil into good.
Come and open our tomorrow
   for a kingdom now so near;
take away all human sorrow –
   give us hope in place of fear.

Jaci Maraschin, Brazil

130 Your people tremble, wonder and are perplexed
as they see their nation grappling with creeping materialism,
atheism and gnawing corruption in high and low places.
Grant your Church strength, wisdom and courage
to confront the people of this nation,
and announce the Good News of eternal life through Jesus Christ.

John Banda, Zambia

Lord of love, moment by moment I encounter men and women 131
whom I do not know, but whose generosity and simple nobility are
plain to see.

Perhaps they are not believers. Perhaps they do not know what I
know. But inwardly I say to them, 'Receive a blessing. You have done
me so much good. I would love to do you a little good in return.'
The good these people have done, without being aware of it, would
I be able to do as well?

But how do I dream of igniting such fires, when all I have in my
hands is poor wood which is damp and green, and spent tapers? I
who am so reluctant to do good in ordinary, everyday things, how
is it possible I should do great and extraordinary deeds?

'My child,' you say to me, Lord, 'what matters is not the little you
hold in your hands. It is to join that little to the fire which is in
my heart. There your tapers will be restored and your wood made
dry. You think that you dare risk almost nothing, but this almost
nothing, if you really try, can become something extraordinary. I
do not say something spectacular. Concentrate on the more ordinary
things, the weaker ones. Do ordinary things in an extraordinary
way. I mean, with extraordinary love. Then the kindling will light.
Then the fire will take hold, will take hold of you. Then you
yourself will begin to be a carrier of fire.'

A monk of the Eastern Orthodox Church

132 Christ Jesus, when multitudes of children and young people, marked for life by being abandoned, are like strangers on this earth, some people ask: 'Does my life still have any meaning?' And you assure us of this: 'Each time you alleviate the suffering of an innocent person, you do it for me, Christ.'

Brother Roger of Taizé, France

133 Lord, strengthen those who are trying to help the apathetic and who are struggling for the underprivileged and discriminated against. When they seem to fail save them from bitterness of spirit, from cynicism, from loss of faith and hope, and when they have success give them humility. Encourage them always to be bold and patient, and fill them with the joy and love which the gift of your Spirit brings; make them realize how much they may learn from those they try to help.

Michael Hollings and Eta Gullick, England

UNITY

O God Eternal, good beyond all that is good, fair beyond all that is   134
fair, in whom is calmness and peace:
reconcile the differences which divide us from one another and
bring us back into the unity of love which may bear some likeness
to your divine nature.
Grant that we may be spiritually one,
both within ourselves and with one another, through the grace,
mercy and tenderness of your Son, Jesus Christ.

an Orthodox prayer

We give thanks and praise to Almighty God for the work within   135
this world through our Lord Jesus Christ, because even in our
divided humanity, separated from each other, we experience now
and then the reconciliation which comes from you; our thanks to
you and praise can never end.

We ask you to accept us in your Son. Grant us the spirit of unity
that takes away whatever comes to divide us. Keep us in union with
all your people and make your Church become a sign of unity
among all people. We pray all this through Jesus Christ, our Lord.

Janet Nyenda, Uganda

136 O God, whose will it is that all your children should be one in Christ, we pray for the unity of your Church. Pardon all our pride and our lack of faith, of understanding and of charity, which are the causes of our divisions. Deliver us from narrow-mindedness, from our bitterness, from our prejudices. Save us from considering as normal that which is a scandal to the world and an offence to your love. Teach us to recognize the gifts of grace among all those who call upon you and confess the faith of Jesus Christ our Lord.

French Reformed Church Liturgy

137   O God, the giver of life,
        we pray for the Church throughout the world:
        sanctify its life; renew its worship;
        empower its witness; restore its unity.
        Remove from your people all pride
        and every prejudice that dulls their will for unity.
        Strengthen the work of all those who strive to seek
        that common obedience that will bind us together.
        Heal the divisions which separate your children from
            one another,
        that they may keep the unity of the Spirit in the
            bond of peace.

*Prayer used in the Ecumenical Centre, Geneva, Switzerland,
on the occasion of the visit of Pope John Paul II*

Let us pray to God who calls us in Jesus Christ to unity: 138

for the Christian Churches on earth: that they may no longer allow themselves to be separated from each other by questions and problems that have often long since ceased to be ours;

for the leaders in our Churches: that like the apostles they may be open to the call of the Spirit, put off all fear and may speak in words all Christians can understand;

for all theologians and ministers: that they may humble themselves under the mighty hand of God and, setting aside human caution and shrewdness, may trust in the Spirit who comes to the aid of our weakness;

for those men and women who can no longer understand the separation of Christians and also for those who equate the Church of Jesus Christ only with their own favourite customs: that they all may recognize that it is not the way back but the way into the future that they tread together which alone can give us unity.

Lord, our God,
lead us through the love of your Son,
our Lord Jesus Christ,
to the unity we long for.

Biddings and Prayers of the Church in Holland

139 Lord Jesus, your sign of reconciliation is the Cross, in all its breadth
and length and height and depth. Teach us to share it with you and
our sisters and brothers so that we may learn to act justly, to walk
humbly, to love tenderly. And so, waiting upon the Spirit, become
instruments of your peace, to the glory of the Father.

The Hengrave Prayer, England

140 Loving God, whose glory outshines the sun, open our lives to the
inspiration of your Holy Spirit that we may fully reflect the glory
of your love and share ourselves with one another in this time of
worship. In Christ's name we pray.

Written for the 6th Assembly of the World Council of Churches, Vancouver

141 Draw your Church together, O Lord, into one great company of
disciples, together following our Lord Jesus Christ into every walk
of life, together serving him in his mission to the world, and together witnessing to his love on every continent and island. We ask this
in his Name and for his sake.

Anglican Church of Canada

God, our Heavenly Father, we draw near to you with thankful 142
hearts because of your great love for us. We thank you most of all
for the gift of your dear Son, in whom alone we may be one. We
are different from one another in race and language, in material
things, in gifts, in opportunities, but each of us has a human heart,
knowing joy and sorrow, pleasure and pain. We are one in our need
of your forgiveness, your strength, your love; make us one in our
response to you, that bound by common love, and freed from selfish
aims, we may work for the good of all and the advancement of your
kingdom.

Women's World Day of Prayer, 1993,
written by women from Guatemala

God our Mother and Father, be with us as we learn to see one 143
another with new eyes, hear one another with new hearts, and treat
one another in a new way.

Corrymeela Community, Ireland

CHRISTIAN LIFE

I am only a spark;
make me a fire.
I am only a string;
make me a lyre.
I am only a drop;
make me a fountain.
I am only an ant hill;
make me a mountain.
I am only a feather;
make me a wing.
I am only a rag;
make me a king!

Unknown, Mexico

THE LIFE OF FAITH

145   Goodness is stronger than evil;
                love is stronger than hate;
                light is stronger than darkness;
                life is stronger than death;
                victory is ours through him who loves us.

Desmond Tutu, South Africa

146 God of every human being, you never force our heart; you place your peaceful light within each one of us. With that light shining on them, our failures and our joys can find meaning in you.

Brother Roger of Taizé, France

147   Lord God, I bring to you:
                My sins for your forgiveness.
                My hopes, my aims, my ambitions for your blessings.
                My temptations for your strength.
                My words and duties and responsibilities for your help.
                My family, friends and all loved ones for your care
                    and protection.
                My sickness for your healing.

Women's World Day of Prayer, 1991,
written by women from Kenya

Thank you, Lord, 148
that your grace
helps us to realize
that rebellion
against weakness, sins, mistakes
is the pride
of those who think themselves perfect
and forget that we are
weakness, weakness, weakness!
Ah! If only our pride understood
that you perform miracles
to sustain
true and genuine humility.

Dom Helder Camara, Brazil

You grant me the clear confidence that you exist, and that you will 149
ensure that not all the ways of goodness are blocked.

Alexander Solzhenitsyn, Russia

Lord, I am afraid of being laughed at because I want to live as I 150
think a Christian should. Never let me give up trying to keep your
laws however people may mock. Never let me laugh at people who
are trying to do right. Lord, it is not easy being your disciple in a
permissive age when conformity to permissiveness is the law of so
many. Give me a clear vision to see what is right and the strength
to do it and take away my fears.

Michael Hollings and Eta Gullick, England

151 Christ Jesus, when we think we are alone, you are there. If there
seems to be doubt within us, that does not make you love us any
the less. We would like to be daring enough to take risks on account
of you, Christ. So we pay attention to your words: 'Whoever gives
his life for love of me will find it.'

Brother Roger of Taizé, France

152   One unforgettable day, dear God
            You reached down to where I was
            And lifted me up to where you are
            And we have been inseparable
            From that moment to this.

Ruth Harms Calkin, Pakistan

153 For your blessing we thank you, God.
Faith in you, increase it, we beg, so that we no longer doubt.
Drive out all our miserliness, so that we do not refuse you anything.
Increase our faith, for the sake of those without faith.
Make us instruments of your faith, for those with only a little.
Fill our bodies with faith, our bodies that work for you all our days.
Help us to avoid the enemies of our faith, or to overcome them.
You are with us in confrontations; this we believe.
In your hands we place ourselves, and are secure.
Make haste to enter our hearts; make haste.

Masai people, Tanzania

Look at me with mercy, O God, 154
as I meditate to know and love you more and more.
I call on you for your guidance.

Where I have not fulfilled your Commandments,
I humbly kneel down in prayer for forgiveness.
Keep encouraging me, O God,
in all I do to please you.

In your mercy, O God,
where all is peace, I'll be led
not to regret but to rejoice
as in your company I get all my comfort.

Fred R Musimenta, Uganda

Years ago our Elders said, 155
'It is God who drives away flies from the tail-less animal.'
The same God touches each of us with the Spirit of power
to cope and overcome,
to drive away fears and anxieties,
to help us to walk through life in the fire of faith.

Moderator of the Evangelical Presbyterian Church in Ghana

156   God, tender and strong,
           as the plover defends her young
           against their enemies,
        so defend me
           against those anxieties and nameless fears
           which are my enemies.
        Save me in the hour of trial,
           and deliver me from evil.
        Under your wings
           let me shelter
        until faith and courage return:
        for your love's sake.

Bruce D Prewer, Australia

157   Just as the fawn stays in the undergrowth, some way from
       the clearing,
    because its life is threatened from moment to moment,
    so may we keep attentive to everything which gives life
       its quality,
    and to everything which, swiftly or slowly, can destroy it.

Stany Simon SJ, France

Unsleeping friend,   158
when I come to the end of my strength,
and my work has no blessing in it,
help me to remember you,
to reach for the hand of a friend
and find your love is here.

Bernard Thorogood, United Kingdom

Jesus, be our peace. You never want us to experience the upheavals   159
of spiritual desolation. When we realise that everything depends
upon our trusting in your love, we listen to your call: 'By the Holy
Spirit, make yourself a heart that is determined to welcome everything in the radiance of praise.'

Brother Roger of Taizé, France

LIFE'S JOURNEY

160 God of many names,
my name is known to you.
I am held in the hand of your life,
and I do not know what you will make of me.
All I know is that I cannot make myself
any more than I could in my mother's womb.
But this I can do,
this I choose,
to give myself into the hand of your continuing
  creativity.
My past, with its joys and triumphs, its failures and
  regrets.
My present, with its struggles and accomplishments, its
  failures and regrets.
My future, with its fears and freedom, its pain and
  promise.
To loose and to bind, to stretch and to shape,
to become what I will,
trusting the hand that made the world
trusting the spirit that breathes life
trusting the love that will not let me go
trusting the promise of the Word made flesh.

Kathy Galloway, Scotland

God of all time,   161
who makes all things new,
we bring before you the year now ending.
For life full and good,
for opportunities recognised and taken,
for love known and shared,
we thank you.

Where we have fallen short,
forgive us.
When we worry over what is past,
free us.

As we begin again
and take our first few steps into the future,
where nothing is safe and certain,
except you,
we ask for the courage of the wise men
who simply went and followed a star.
We ask for their wisdom,
in choosing to pursue the deepest truth,
not knowing where they would be led.

In the year to come, God of all time,
be our help and company.
Hold our hands as we journey onwards
and may your dream of shalom,
where all will be at peace,
be our guiding star.

Francis Brienen, United Kingdom

162   Eternal God,
We say good morning to you.
Hallowed be your name.
Early in the morning, before we begin our work,
we praise your glory.
Renew our bodies as fresh as the morning flowers.
Open our inner eyes, as the sun casts new light upon
    the darkness
which prevailed over the night.
Deliver us from all captivity.
Give us wings of freedom like the birds in the sky,
to begin a new journey.
Restore justice and freedom, as a mighty stream
running continuously as day follows day.
We thank you for the gift of this morning,
and a new day to work with you.

Masao Takenaka, Japan

163 O God, you have prepared in peace the path I must follow today. Help me to walk straight on that path. If I speak, remove lies from my lips. If I am hungry, take away from me all complaint. If I have plenty, destroy pride in me. May I go through the day calling on you, you, O Lord, who know no other Lord.

Galla people, Ethiopia

The poor and the weak have revealed to me   164
the great secret of Jesus.
If you wish to follow him
you must not try to climb the ladder of success and power,
becoming more and more important.
Instead, you must walk *down* the ladder,
to meet and walk with people
who are broken and in pain.
The light is there, shining in the darkness,
the darkness of their poverty.
The poor with whom you are called to share your life
are the sick and the old;
people out of work,
young people caught up in the world of drugs,
people angry because they were terribly hurt
when they were young,
people with disabilities or sick with AIDS,
or just out of prison . . .
people who are oppressed
because of the colour of their skin . . .
people in pain.

Jean Vanier, Canada

Christ Jesus, following you is discovering this Gospel reality: you are   165
praying within each one of us. Your forgiveness and your presence
bring to birth the clarity of trust and you offer an inner healing.

Brother Roger of Taizé, France

166   Our brother Jesus, you set our feet upon the way and sometimes
        where you lead we do not like or understand.
     Bless us with courage where the way is fraught with dread
        or danger;
     bless us with graceful meetings where the way is lonely;
     bless us with good companions where the way demands a
        common cause;
     bless us with night vision where we travel in the dark, keen
        hearing where we have not sight, to hear the reassuring
        sounds of fellow travellers;
     bless us with humour – we cannot travel lightly weighed
        down with gravity;
     bless us with humility to learn from those around us;
     bless us with decisiveness where we must move with speed;
     bless us with lazy moments, to stretch and rest and savour;
     bless us with love, given and received;
     and bless us with your presence, even when we know it
        in your absence.
     Lead us into exile,
     until we find that on the road
        is where you are,
     and where you are is going home.
     Bless us, lead us, love us, bring us home
        bearing the Gospel of life.

                                        Kathy Galloway, Scotland

O Jesus, be the canoe that holds me up in the sea of life;   167
be the rudder that helps me in the straight road;
be the outrigger that supports me in times of temptation;
let your Spirit be my sail that carries me through each day.
Keep my body strong, so I can paddle steadfastly on in the
voyage of life.

Church of the Province of Melanesia

O God, slow us down and help us to see that we are put in charge 168
of our lives, but with your help. Help us to get in tune with the
rhythm that makes for life.

We keep moving, even though we know that we are made to
center down, as well as to be actively engaged in the business of life.
We compete for things and make those things more important than
they ought to be. We eat what we ought not to eat. We neglect and
misuse our bodies. We fail to discipline our minds and to be still and
know that you are God and that we are the temple of the Most
High. Yet we often complain about our misfortunes and our hard
luck, when at times it is we who are guilty of disregard.

Help us to know that we can be broken by life only if we first
allow the victory of evil over our spirits.

May our hope and strength and faith be grounded in you; and
may we recall the strength of our model, our Brother and your Son.

George Thomas, United States

169   Soft the Master's love song,
and beautiful to hear:
'Come to me, you poor,
all who stumble in distress;
relief from toil I offer,
come to me for rest.'

'If you're burdened down,
let me bear the strain for you.
You must not despair:
through my Easter death has died;
so journey on with courage,
I am by your side.'

Jesus you are strong,
I am weak, a foolish child;
I will turn to you,
boast in you alone, my friend.
Your words give life to live by,
love that has no end.

Rudolf Pantou, Indonesia

170   Disturbing God,
you identify with the weak and powerless,
and surprise us as we seek to do your will.
Help us to find true hope
in the now of our action
rather than in the distant future of our longing.

Joy Tetley, England

God, there are corners in my soul 171
that I don't know yet.
How can I ever understand myself?
How can I ever fathom
my answer to the challenge of life?
Where are you?
Are you possibly present
in those unknown corners?
Lighten up what is hidden,
reveal my soul,
untie your secret in me.
I would like
to meet the others
with only light in my eyes,
with an unbiased heart.
I would like to be an oasis
in the desert of life,
a home where they can rest,
a tree in whose shade
they can finally meet you.

André Quintelier, Philippines

172

Lord, let us
put our ear to the ground
and listen,
hurried, worried footsteps,
bitterness, rebellion.
Hope
hasn't yet begun.
Listen again.
Put out feelers.
You are there.
You are far less likely
to abandon us
in hardship
than in times of ease.

Dom Helder Camara, Brazil

173

Father, we are pilgrims of eternity.
We stand before you.
Let us not seek to deaden the desire for you
which disturbs our hearts.
Let us rather yield ourselves to its constraints
and go where it leads us.
Give us the courage to make sacrifices,
to yield our past to you
and our future.
Then use us, in Christ's name, to be bearers
of freedom to slaves and prisoners
and joy to broken hearts.

Church Army, England

Almighty and eternal God, ruler of the universe, ever present 174
around, beneath, above and within me, behold, I come to do your
will, O God. I know not what to do. My mind is darkened. My will
is weak. I am weary and lonely and I ask again, 'Lord, what will you
have me to do?'

I find the circumstances of my life hard, at times, O God. I do
not understand why things happen the way they do. Then, I
remember your divine Son, Jesus Christ, as his soul was sorrowful
unto death. In the garden he sweat his precious blood in agony and
found the divine will of his heavenly Father difficult. And he prayed
– Lord Jesus, you prayed! – 'Not my will, but yours be done.'

Robert J Fox, United States

Lord 175
may I ever speak
as though it were the last word that I can speak.
May I ever act
as though it were the last action that I can perform.

May I ever suffer
as though it were the last pain that I can offer.
May I ever pray
as though it were for me on earth
the last chance to speak to you.

Chiara Lubich, founder of The Focolare Movement, Italy

Penitence,

Forgiveness and

Reconciliation

Lord, 176
if this day you have to correct us,
put us right not out of anger
but with a mother and father's love.
So may we your children
be kept free of falseness and foolishness.

Unknown, Mexico

Lord Jesus, 177
we cannot do anything
without you;
and you yourself
cannot act in us
without our cooperation.

We thank you
for being able to do so much;
but, at the same time,
we see our basic inability
to live up to the fullness of your love.

Save us!
Make us welcome your salvation,
not as a chance to better our lives,
but as the only source of freedom,
without which we cannot break
every last bond
that keeps us enslaved
to ourselves.

Pierre Talec, France

178   Lord, you see my sins more clearly
      than I can myself;
      you know when I am untruthful
      and when I think evil of others.
      You see my anger
      and unfairness to my friends.
      You know how hard it is for me to forgive.

      Lord, you know
      when I am indifferent
      to your Word, the Bible;
      how often I forget
      to pray;
      the times I come unwillingly
      to worship;
      and yet I turn to you,
      when I am in trouble.

      Lord, I have sinned,
      without considering how much
      you love me.

      Forgive me and make me clean,
      so that I can obey your call
      to take up your cross
      and follow you.

Maureen Edwards, Kenya

Lord, forgive us,   179
for we are fragmented persons.
We go many directions at once.
We seek opposite goals;
we serve contradictory causes.
We mouth liberation, we live oppression.
We shout peace, we practise
violence and anarchy.
We shout justice, we walk in injustice.
We preach love, we practise hate.
Through your compassion
have mercy on us and make us whole.
Enable us to discern your voice
among the dissonant voices.

Unknown writer, Philippines

I have not yet reached the shore where there is no hatred,   180
the clouds of unjust struggles have not yet passed.
The scars of wounds endured have not yet closed,
warm trust in man lies totally dead.
From the springs of forgetting I have not drunk wisdom,
weary memories still poison me.
From the glades of forgiveness I am still distant,
from the sanctuary of refuge I am a great way separated.
Lord, bring me the clear dawn of other days,
may all painful shadows depart from me.
Let me look with tender emotion on the scars of my wounds,
and with meek goodness upon the faces of my enemies.
Bring me the dawn whilst the way is so long,
but do not hinder my striving until I reach the shore.

Traian Dors, Romania

181 Heavenly Father, creator of all things, who rejoiced in your creation at the beginning of the world; forgive us our sins of greed, selfishness and carelessness by which we daily damage the beauty to which we have become insensitive.

By war and violence we destroy families and their means of livelihood. We cut down great forests that are the homes of people, animals and birds. We ill-treat our farm animals in the race to outstrip our rivals in food production, yet still leave millions of people starving. We pollute our air and water with the excess of our greed, without thought for the disposal of what we waste.

For all this we ask not only forgiveness, but also the power to turn away from our headlong course of destruction, and instead to share in your constant work of creation, in preparation for the time when your kingdom comes to earth as it is in heaven.

This we ask through Jesus Christ, our Saviour, who himself became part of your creation and gave his life for the whole world.

Helen Lamb, Ireland

182   Forgive us when we forget to praise you,
         when we turn your love into legalism,
         your freedom into slavery,
         your promises and gifts into demands and duties.
         Forgive us when we forget we are your people
         and we make your Church an exclusive club;
         forgive us when we forget that Jesus is our
         contemporary and we lock him up in forms and customs,
         words and structures.
         Forgive us, merciful God.

from Methodist induction service, Aotearoa (New Zealand)

Almighty God, forgive our selfishness 183
and lack of understanding of other nations.
Forgive our indifference to the many who are not free,
and even suffer martyrdom for their faith.
Forgive, O God, our poor stewardship
of the resources you have so generously given us.
Forgive our disregard of the painful struggle of the few
on behalf of the many
who suffer oppression and neglect.

Women's World Day of Prayer, 1988

Eternal God 184
we confess to you our sinfulness.
You made the world a paradise
but we have turned our lands into
places of tears and unhappiness.
People are fighting with each other
race against race.
The holocaust of chauvinism
sweeps through countries
devouring humanity
terrorising us into submission.

Liberating One
free us from all bondage
so that our faith in you
will make us free
to create with courage
a new world –
new societies.

Sri Lanka

185   Lord, you placed me in the world
            to be its salt.
      I was afraid of committing myself,
      afraid of being stained by the world.
      I did not want to hear what 'they' might say.
      And my salt dissolved as if in water.
      Forgive me, Jesus.

      Lord, you placed me in the world
            to be its light.
      I was afraid of the shadows,
      afraid of the poverty.
      I did not want to know other people.
      And my light slowly faded away.
      Forgive me, Jesus.

      Lord, you placed me in the world
            to live in community.
      Thus you taught me to love,
      to share in life,
      to struggle for bread and for justice,
      your truth incarnate in my life.
      So be it, Jesus.

Peggy M de Cuehlo, Uruguay

186   O Lord, be gracious unto us! In all that we hear or see, in all that
      we say or do, be gracious unto us. I ask pardon of the Great God. I
      ask pardon at the sunset, when every sinner turns to Him. Now and
      forever I ask pardon of God. O Lord, cover us from our sins, guard
      our children and protect our weaker friends.

Camel driver's prayer, country unknown

You asked for my hands
that you might use them for your purpose.
I gave them for a moment then withdrew them
for the work was hard.

187

You asked for my mouth
to speak out against injustice.
I gave you a whisper that I might not be accused.

You asked for my eyes
to see the pain of poverty.
I closed them for I did not want to see.

You asked for my life
that you might work through me.
I gave a small part that I might not get too involved.

Lord, forgive my calculated efforts to serve you,
only when it is convenient for me to do so,
only in those places where it is safe to do so,
and only with those who make it easy to do so.

Father, forgive me,
renew me
send me out
as a usable instrument
that I might take seriously
the meaning of your cross.

Joe Seremane, South Africa

188   Brothers and sisters, in the presence of the God of glory,
We need to confess our true human condition.
In the light of Christ's self-giving life,
   his way of the Cross,
We see the darkness in our lives.

As we think of the evil and oppression in the world
   of which we are a part,
We need to repent together with our fellow-humans.

As members of a people called to follow Christ
and live in his new righteousness,
We need to repent for the evil in the Church's life.

The Saviour of the world, the Refuge of the repentant,
forgives and strengthens all who truly seek his grace.
He accepts you as his sons and daughters,
and sets you free from the bondage of your past.
For Christ died and rose to new life that we might all share his
wholeness and abundant life.

Church of South India

189 O Lord Jesus Christ, Son of the living God, forgive us the many
times we have judged others without knowing or loving them.
Give us an awareness of our sins and shortcomings and make us see
ourselves as you know us. Guide us in all our contacts with those
around us and fill us with mercy and love; through Jesus Christ our
Lord.

Church Army, England

O God, only you know the truth of the burden 190
which each of us carries.
We know that some of the burdens
which we wish to lay down
can be picked up by the gifts and energy of others.
Sometimes we can be so supported by others
that the things we are carrying seem lighter.
Sometimes we can change our life in ways
which bring new justice and care.
For other things, we have few answers,
too few resources in ourselves
to bring in the changes,
or we simply fail in what we would hope to do or be.

For this we grieve.
For this we pray forgiveness.
For all, we pray for new ways
to journey on in hope.

Dorothy McRae-McMahon, Australia

We have learned from you that we should treat others 191
    as we would have others treat us.
Why is this one of the most difficult lessons in all
    of life for us to comprehend?
We continue to withhold love.
We deny mercy.
We steel ourselves against compassion.
Most of us will one day grow old, God.
Will we then be treated with love, mercy, and compassion?

Malcolm Boyd, United States

192   Lord God of heaven, you are great and we stand in awe of you. You faithfully keep your new covenant with those people who trust in you and in Jesus Christ, whom you have sent. Look down on us, Lord, and hear our prayers as we pray for your Church here in this nation. We confess that we, your people, have sinned. We and all the people of this nation have gone away from you and your Gospel, the Good News about Jesus Christ.

Remember now what you have done in him and not what we deserve. For his sake renew and restore your people, rebuild your Church and win this nation for Christ and his Gospel once again.

We ask this in his name and for your honour and glory.

Crosswinds, England

193   Loving and good God, how great your love and goodness are to us. Out of your love you extend your grace, and reward those who do not deserve it. It is out of your love that we are not crushed, but able to survive the challenges surrounding us. You extend your love to the unlovable – to rejected, hopeless sinners. Because your love and goodness know no boundaries, you dine with both black and white. Because your love and goodness know no discrimination, rich and refugees, orphans and street children, learned and illiterate, all are called by your name; and you call us all your children.

    Lord, how great is your love and goodness to us. You love all who are neglected and rejected. So we say thank you, Lord, for your love and goodness to us and to the whole world.

Lazarus M Katiso, Kenya

Lord Jesus Christ, you are the way of peace. 194
Come into the brokenness of our lives and our land with your healing love.
Help us to be willing to bow before you in true repentance, and to bow to one another in real forgiveness.
By the fire of your Holy Spirit, melt our hard hearts and consume the pride and prejudice which separate us.
Fill us, O Lord, with your perfect love which casts out fear and bind us together in that unity which you share with the Father and the Holy Spirit.

A prayer used in the Irish Republic and in Northern Ireland

God, we believe that you have called us together 195
to broaden our experience of you and of each other.
We believe that we have been called
to help in healing the many wounds of society
and in reconciling man to man and man to God.
Help us, as individuals or together,
to work, in love, for peace, and never to lose heart.
We commit ourselves to each other –
in joy and sorrow.
We commit ourselves to all who share our belief in
   reconciliation –
to support and stand by them.
We commit ourselves to the way of peace –
in thought and deed.
We commit ourselves to you –
as our guide and friend.

Corrymeela Community, Ireland

MARRIAGE, HOME AND FAMILY

Lord, it is utterly wonderful being in love. The whole world looks 196
different; it is transformed, joyous, and shining. I cannot thank you
enough for letting this happen to me. Never let me fall out of love.
I know the way of loving must change, must deepen, perhaps even
become less obviously joyful, but please make it endure. Help me
always to be considerate and understanding, and stop me from caus-
ing pain to the one I love. I ask this in the name of your son, Jesus.

Michael Hollings and Eta Gullick, England

Almighty God, you introduced the mystery that a man and a woman 197
should live together as husband and wife, leaving their parents to
become one. We thank you, Lord, for your fatherly care and for
making it possible for our sons and daughters to marry. For as much
as without you we cannot do anything, we ask you to make their
homes full of peace and love. Bless them with good children. Now
that they have married their husbands and wives they are our sons
and daughters. Make us loving and faithful fathers and mothers to
our sons- and daughters-in-law. Father, send your Holy Spirit into
the hearts of our sons- and daughters-in-law; and increase their love
so that they will accept us as fathers- and mothers-in-law, even as
their own mothers and fathers. Help us to be enduring, understanding, merciful and kind; and to live together peacefully in the
name of our Lord, Jesus Christ.

Hannah Aduke Haruma, Nigeria

198   For the day of our marriage
and the years we have shared together,
we praise and thank you, Lord.

For faithfulness and friendship,
for love and security,
we praise and thank you, Lord.

For the hours of happiness and joy,
for the hours of sadness and tears,
we praise and thank you, Lord.

For difficulties shared
and problems overcome,
we praise and thank you, Lord.

For your gift of children,
and all that you have blessed us with,
we praise and thank you, Lord.

For your protecting power,
and your presence in our home,
we praise and thank you, Lord.

For the love you have shown us,
and your peace and grace given us,
we praise and thank you, Lord.

Almighty and heavenly Father,
for all that lies ahead of us
we trust and praise you.

For the future together without fear,
we trust and praise you.

For our love to deepen and strengthen,
we trust and praise you.

For the anticipation of grandchildren,
we trust and praise you.

For the hope in which we look to you,
we trust and praise you.

For the salvation we have in you,
we trust and praise you.

Pamela Wilding, Kenya

In the stillness of this moment I hold my breath, and marvel at the   199
wonder of this second chance in marriage.

God, thank you for this second time of marriage. We each accept
all that has gone before. We pledge ourselves to this new love. May
our experiences and differences take on a positive value, that through
them we may enrich our lives as we learn from one another.

Thank you for our past, for the pains and for the joys.

Thank you for your blessing on us now. May we continue to
know this blessing and may it always be part of our lives together.

Joined in Love, Aotearoa (New Zealand)

200   Generous Father,
you made the human family to be
the simplest unit of society.
It is a communion of minds and hearts,
the cradle of the Church,
the foundation of the community.

Bless, prosper and watch over
the well-being of my family.
Preserve and foster our mutual love and respect.
Unite us, above all, in striving
to know, love and serve you.
Help us to be
of benefit to society
and to your Church, to advance your Good News
and proclaim your holiness.
Help us all to grow closer to you
and to one another.

Lawrence Gandiya, Zimbabwe

201 May your blessing rest on the new home whose life begins today.
Sanctify it with your presence, and fill it with peace and love;
through Jesus Christ our Lord.

Lord bless us and protect us.
Lord, smile on us and show us your favour.
Lord, befriend us and prosper us.

Ruth Etchells, England

Come, Lord Jesus,   202
into my heart and home.
You are a welcome guest.
Feast at my table,
drink of my wine.
Thank you for your friendship.
Please stay with me
now and always.

Josephine Bax, England

Good Lord,   203
   just as you were pleased to relax,
   in the home of Martha and Mary,
   abide also, we pray, in our homes.

We pray, especially, for those homes of this congregation,
   where we meet together,
   for prayer,
   for fellowship,
   and Bible study.

Bestow upon them an atmosphere of Christian love,
   where your presence can be found,
   your Word made known,
   your will accepted
   and your purpose worked out.

William N Richards and James Richardson, Kenya

204 Almighty God, we thank you for the gift of children and for the women who are pregnant. We pray you bless all the pregnant women and we pray that you give them faith and hope.

Give strength to those who are weak and especially those who live in villages and far from ante-natal clinics. Give wisdom to the traditional birth attendants who care for them; give them love and ability so that they are able to help the pregnant women.

We pray all this through Jesus Christ, our Lord.

Four women from Uganda

205   I haven't much to offer as I'm not very rich,
       But God gave me a gift of love so I've put some in each
          stitch.
       So when you wrap it round your child with care and
          tender love,
       I pray that God will clothe your child forever in his love.

Marjorie Andrews, Wales

206 For Mary, Mother of Jesus, we give you thanks and praise, O Lord. We thank you for her example of trust in you, and for her obedience to your will.

We praise you, O Lord, for her spirit of acceptance, and for her care and love for the child of Bethlehem.

We give you thanks that she was able to stand by the cross and to be with him in death as she was in birth.

We give you thanks for John's acceptance of her as his own mother, leaving us an example of care.

Church Army, England

Lord Jesus, friend of little children, I thank you for what you do to 207
make little children happy in their play, in their work at school and
at home. I praise you for your love and glory. I ask that they are
purified, enlightened and inspired as they grow in your light to
serve in the community in which they find themselves. I pray you
help them in your holiness and truth so that they can be useful
citizens in service to their families and their nation.

Joanna Cofie, Gambia

He looks so little as he struggles up the high steps   208
    of the school bus!

Please, Lord, reach down and give him a boost –
    the first of many he'll need
    through the big steps and high climbs
    of future lessons in living!

Thanks, Lord, for being there to help when I can't be.

Mary Sue H Rosenberger, United States

My God, have mercy on our children   209
who were late in getting up.
My God, do not lead our children to ruin.
My God, our life is in our children.
My God, give us children, both small and big.
My God, be the guardian of our children
that are away in order to feed our cattle
in any grassland.
My God, I am old and near death
and my house needs help.
You be the guardian of all creatures.
Let it be so, my God.
Answer kindly to the words that we,
a group of elders, have said to you.
And God answered affirmatively.

Samburu people, Kenya

210

I saw it this morning, Lord,
   that unspoiled, open
   innocence of youth.
Clean, honest,
   and naked on the world:
   my son, Lord, my son.
And, for a fleeting moment
   it was me
   (how many years ago?)
   with lines and shadows scrubbed away.
Gone, too, the sophistication
   that so often covers childlike things
   like fear
   and awe
   and love.
God, in your forgiveness,
   give me innocence again,
   just once,
   again.

Ken Thompson, United States

VOCATION

O Lord, our heavenly Father, we commend to your protecting care 211
and compassion the men and women of this and every land now
suffering distress and anxiety through lack of work. Prosper, we
pray, the counsel of those engaged in the order of industrial life, that
all people may be set free from want and fear, and may be enabled
to work in security and peace, for the happiness of the common life
and the wellbeing of their countries. Through Jesus Christ, our
Lord.

Women from the Llandaff diocese, Wales

O God, I don't find much contentment in my job.   212
It is so difficult to believe
that this is your will for my life.
Grant me the courage and the strength
to do the hard things today
and to do them well.
I am going to face things
that I can't handle by myself.
I know the promises concerning your presence,
but help me to feel something of that presence
in the difficult hours of this day.

Leslie F Brandt, United States

213 Back in Palestine, Jesus,
    I guess nobody had to meet deadlines.
  Now everybody's in a rush.
    Every week needs two Fridays.
    Every month an extra week.
  I meet most of them, Jesus,
    but it causes me to
    treat people in ways I don't like.
    (And it causes me to treat myself
    in a way that's killing, too.)
  Mary and Joseph were meeting deadlines, though,
    weren't they?
    The time to be taxed.
    The time to give you birth.
    – 'The fullness of time . . .'
  They did it.
    And in a stable!
  Jesus, help me to get a better perspective
    of time
    and priorities
    and your coming again.

Ken Thompson, United States

Lord, help us to resist the temptation 214
which money presents.

Help those with financial problems and debts
to avoid dishonest and corrupt ways.

Help us all not to be influenced
by the materialistic standards
of other countries.
Help us not to envy
those who are better off than ourselves.
Help us to close the gap
between rich and poor
in our own country.

Guide all managers and directors
of large business concerns,
that they may have steadiness of purpose
and do what is lawful and right.

Strengthen our faith and courage
to face evil and corruption.

Maureen Edwards, Kenya

215   Lord God,
        help us to control inflation.
           It plays havoc with the economy,
           destroys all incentive to plan and save
           and causes us all such anxiety.

        Overrule our greed,
           so that just profits are received,
           fair wages paid,
           and reasonable prices charged.

        Show us how to reward hard work and responsibility
           and to ensure that no-one has less than he needs
           to feed and care for himself and his family.

William N Richards and James Richardson, Kenya

216 O Jesus Christ, you knew the workshop of Joseph and you saw the sweat of the labourer. Bless those who work and those who employ workers. May your Church, the steward of your way of life, teach us how to labour honestly and how to reward work justly. Help us to uphold the dignity of human labour, that whether in physical or mental work the person is more important than the job. Guide those who make decisions about employment and payment; temper our discussions about money and work with a sense that we are your servants, that we may be motivated neither by a greed for money nor by a desire to get as much as we can for as little pay as possible. May we seek the welfare of each other, remembering that we all have but one Master who is also our Judge and our Saviour, even the same Jesus Christ.

Ralston Smith, Jamaica

Father,   217

we give our thanks for the men and women
  who go on doing their duty
  in the face of
  loneliness,
  monotony,
  misunderstanding,
  danger.

We pray for those who serve us in this city
  at hazard to their lives:
  the policemen and firemen
  and all others whose work demands constant risk.

We pray for the soldiers and sailors
  who at any moment are either bored or scared,
  but they stay at their post and do what they must.
  Father, bless their courage
  with the peace that they, and we, are praying for.

Forgive us, Father,
  if we ever take for granted what others are doing
  so that we can live in peace and safety.
  Make us the kind of people who deserve these blessings.

We expect others to show courage in the line of duty.
  If, once in a while,
  we must stand up to be counted
  and show a little courage of our own,
  help us to set them an example
  by being the kind of people Christ has called us to be.

Andrew W Blackwood Jr, United States

218   Bless, O Father, our citizens,
whose lives are lived in the towns
and whose work is done in shops, offices and factories.

Provide for them fit places in which to work and live
and decent places of entertainment.

Safeguard the moral standards of young people,
who come unprepared for urban life.

Steer us away from crime and violence
and the dangers and temptations associated with big cities.

And give life to our cathedrals and town parishes,
to our community centres,
and industrial chaplains,
that they might be really involved in the daily life
of our people.

William N Richards and James Richardson, Kenya

Gentle, compassionate God,   219
I weep for my sisters –
women in joy, women in pain,
unsure of who they are as humans,
unsure of who they are as women . . . unsure.

They work so hard, too hard,
trying to hold it all together.
They long for the sweet gentleness of love;
tender, loving, caring gentleness;
and receive a different kind of love –
off-handed, well-meaning, rough yet genuine.
This love is rarely expressed in a way that really touches
their inner needs, their inner longing.

They struggle to come to terms with unfulfilled relationships;
with being the main child-carer, child-raiser;
being locked into the smallness of a country community;
being wife, mother, housewife, farm worker, economic expert.
God, they are beautiful women,
hurting women,
longing, aching, needing women.

They have such courage,
so many inner resources and strengths;
I am in awe of them.

I rejoice in my sisters in the country;
I weep for my sisters.
I weep for my sisters.

Noel Nicholls, Australia

220   Dear Lord, the office is so quiet at this hour.
Arriving early
    has brought a dimension to things
    I seldom see when the tempo picks up.
Now, while it's quiet
    and this whole day lies before me
    unopened and unspoiled,
    help me to remember
    what tranquility is
    (and how it remains
    hidden under shouts
    and bells
    and knocks
    and confusion).
Let me reach back during the day today
    and get the strength I feel right now
    from the knowledge
    that there is peace in your world
    (even when we hide it
    in brief moments
    not at all like these).

Ken Thompson, United States

221   God of heaven and earth,
    artist and artisan,
    free us to see things afresh,
    that we may be fully alive
    and truly for your glory.

Joy Tetley, England

HEALTH
AND SICKNESS

Dearest Lord, may I see you today and every day in the person of 222 your sick, and whilst nursing minister to you.

Though you hide yourself behind the unattractive disguise of the irritable, the exacting, the unreasonable, may I still recognize you and say: 'Jesus, my patient, how sweet it is to serve you.'

Lord, give me this seeing faith, then my work will never be monotonous. I will ever find joy in humouring the fancies and gratifying the wishes of all poor sufferers.

O beloved sick, how doubly dear you are to me, when you personify Christ; and what a privilege is mine to be allowed to tend you.

Sweetest Lord, make me appreciative of the dignity of my high vocation, and its many responsibilities. Never permit me to disgrace it by giving way to coldness, unkindness, or impatience.

And, O God, while you are Jesus, my patient, deign also to be to me a patient Jesus, bearing with my faults, looking only to my intention, which is to love and serve you in the person of each of your sick.

Lord, increase my faith, bless my efforts and work, now and for evermore.

Mother Teresa of India (her daily prayer)

223 Most heavenly Father of the human race, behold me, unworthy though I am; see that I am about to have a baby. I pray that you assist me to bear the pain of childbirth courageously, and give me physical and moral strength. Avert from me any unseen or unnatural circumstance and grant me the privilege of bearing a normal, healthy baby. Hear my humble prayer, dear Lord, offered to you with confidence and love in this hour of my expectation. Help me to be a good mother in word and example. Grant that after my delivery my little baby may learn at an early age of your greatness. May the joy and peace of a safe delivery fill my heart, and may your blessed name be praised now and for evermore.

Sister E Gbonda, Sierra Leone

224 Give me a candle of the Spirit, O God, as I go down into the deeps of my being. Show me the hidden things, the creatures of my dreams, the storehouse of forgotten memories and hurts. Take me down to the spring of my life, and tell me my nature and my name. Give me freedom to grow, so that I may become that self, the seed of which you planted in me at my making. Out of the deeps I cry to you, O God.

George Appleton, England

225
Dear Lord Jesus,
I don't know who I am,
I don't know what I am,
I don't know where I am,
but please love me.

Prayer of a woman suffering from Alzheimer's Disease

We commend to the care and mercy of our Lord Jesus Christ all 226
who have fallen into the power of substances which cause ruin and
misery.

We pray for all those who feel that the 'real world' is so frighten-
ing that it must be obliterated by means of alcohol or drugs.

We pray for all who resort to the use of alcohol to cover their
inadequacy in facing the demands of life; for those who are so
unhappy that they seek a false jollity through heavy drinking.

We commend to the love of God those people, particularly
young people, who are slaves to drugs, which stimulate the senses
or depress the mind. For those who are now addicts, we pray that
they may not lose all hope or sense of reality.

We bring to the Lord, in our prayers, all those who work with the
frightened people of our society: alcoholics and their families, those
fighting against addiction, and those who have given up the fight.

We pray for those who work in drug addiction units, for doctors,
psychiatrists and social workers; and for those who give themselves
to such a caring.

We ask the Lord to give each one of us the vision and the
strength to live as the free 'slaves of God'; acknowledging the liberty
which this gives to us and showing, by our lives, the joy and fulfil-
ment this brings. Through Jesus Christ our Lord.

Church Army, England

227 Loving God, you show yourself to those who are vulnerable and make your home with the poor and weak of this world.

Warm our hearts with the fire of your Spirit. Help us to accept the challenges of AIDS.

Protect the healthy, calm the frightened, give courage to those in pain, comfort the dying and give to the dead eternal life.

Console the bereaved, strengthen those who care for the sick.

May we your people, using all our energy and imagination, and trusting in your steadfast love, be united with one another in conquering all disease and fear.

Terence Higgins Trust Interfaith Group, United Kingdom

228 Blessed are you, our God, for in Jesus you show us the image of your glory. We give thanks for the gospel of healing and liberation which is preached to the whole Church in the ministry of those with HIV or AIDS. May we recognize that it is the real body of Christ which suffers at this time through HIV and AIDS. It is the real mind of Christ which is racked by fear and confusion. It is the real image of God in Christ which is blasphemed in prejudice, oppression and poverty. May we see in this crisis, loving God, not punishment but the place where God is most powerfully at work in Jesus Christ, and where, as sisters and brothers, we can lead each other to life in all its fullness, given in the same Christ our Lord.

Catholic AIDS Link, United Kingdom

I am praying for my friend who is so very ill. 229
O my Lord, you brought the touch of healing
to those who crossed your path
in your earthly life.
You promised to respond to the prayers
of your children that struggle to follow
and reflect you on this earth.
Reach out now to this one with your healing touch.
She belongs to you, O God.
She yearns so deeply to serve you.
Restore her to life and wholeness once more.
And even while she suffers,
may she sense your nearness
and be embraced by your peace.
Grant that she may have joy
even in the midst of her sufferings.
And grant, blessed Lord,
that she might get well again.

Leslie F Brandt, United States

Journey's End

Master Painter, 230
as the days grow short
  and the chill winds blow
you color the trees more beautifully every day,
    brushing the leaves with brilliant hues
    of reds and golds until
    suddenly
    and quietly
    they fall.

And our lives should be like that, too,
  I think,
for, as the days grow short
  and the bones begin to chill,
you color our days with the brilliant hues
  of experience and wisdom,
but we −
  we miss the beauty and see only the fall,
for, by worshipping the fleeting youth of spring
  we have become blinded to the deep beauty of autumn!

Mary Sue H Rosenberger, United States

231 When the signs of age begin to mark my body (and still more when they touch my mind); when the ill that is to diminish me or carry me off strikes from without or is born within me; when the painful moment comes in which I suddenly awaken to the fact that I am ill or growing old; and above all at that last moment when I feel I am losing hold of myself and am absolutely passive within the hands of the great unknown forces that have formed me; in all those dark moments, O God, grant that I may understand that it is you (provided only my faith is strong enough) who are painfully parting the fibres of my being in order to penetrate to the very marrow of my substance and bear me away within yourself.

Teilhard de Chardin, France

232 Our Father, as years advance and I cannot do the things I once did, help me to change the focus, as I do with my camera, from sweeping panoramas to the beauty of things seen close. Help me to enjoy the flowers on the windowsill as I loved a garden; the birds at the feeder as the birds I used to walk to see on country roads; the play on television, when theater was once a joy; the cup of coffee with a friend instead of a party; my small, cozy rooms instead of the old house. Help me to realize that enjoyment resides not in things, but in my attitude toward them. Grant, I pray, the power to find uncommon joy in common things.

Josephine Robertson, United States

Now I am old, Lord. 233
Only – if anyone looks at me with pity, they are making
    a mistake;
I see further than I used to,
and know more clearly every year
which way my path is headed.
People and things appear from a different perspective,
and sometimes I trace a more roundabout route
    through this crowded earth.
Yet on my best days I feel like the child I used to be,
who went about on stilts from sheer exuberance.
People can laugh if they like,
so long as they do not laugh at me
when I do not always succeed in these endeavours.
I would like to keep busy for a little while yet.
When I get out of breath, then I can let myself rest a little,
and release my grip on a few of the things I have held
    onto tightly up to now,
and then go full of hope towards my final home.

Ingeborg Warnke, Germany, written on a birthday in later life

I ask your compassion on one who is groping, like a traveler, 234
through a thick fog of confusion. Remembering the quick spirit,
the purposeful activity of this person in former years, we who love
him come to you in sorrow. May those who take care of him have
patience, gentleness, and perception. If it be your will, restore him
to the recognition of people and life around him. If this is not to
be, grant that his spirit may be untroubled and that his dreams may
be sweet. With our love we commend this dear soul to you.

Josephine Robertson, United States

235 O God, we remember not only our son but also his murderers; not because they killed him in the prime of his youth and made our hearts bleed and our tears flow, not because with this savage act they have brought further disgrace on the name of our country among the civilized nations of the world; but because through their crime we now follow thy footsteps more closely in the way of sacrifice. The terrible fire of this calamity burns up all selfishness and possessiveness in us; its flame reveals the depth of depravity and meanness and suspicion, the dimension of hatred and the measure of sinfulness in human nature; it makes obvious as never before our need to trust in God's love as shown in the cross of Jesus and his resurrection; love which makes us free from hate towards our persecutors; love which brings patience, forbearance, courage, loyalty, humility, generosity, greatness of heart; love which more than ever deepens our trust in God's final victory and his eternal designs for the Church and for the world; love which teaches us how to prepare ourselves to face our own day of death.

O God, our son's blood has multiplied the fruit of the Spirit in the soil of our souls; so when his murderers stand before thee on the day of judgement remember the fruit of the Spirit by which they have enriched our lives. And forgive.

Bishop Hassan Dehqani-Tafti, Iran, after the murder of his son

O Lord, I felt such terrible disappointment and sadness when they 236
told me my baby had died. I felt so different from all the other
mothers. He had been part of my body for all those months, and
now he is gone. I wanted to hold him, to feel his warm body in my
arms. I wanted to love him. I never had a chance to tell him how
much I loved him. I have only cried for him, missing him.

And then I thought of you, Lord. I knew he was safe with you.
You will love him in such a special way, you will care for him in
your heaven. I feel he is safe, Lord. I still miss him, and sometimes
when I am alone I cry for him and long for him. But that terrible
loneliness is not there when I think that he is at home with you.

Ann Murphy, Wales

God our heavenly Father, Lord of peace, God of love, we pray you 237
guide all children who have lost their parents and are living in hard
times. Lead them in everything they do, send your love into the
hearts of those caring for them. Let this group know your love for
them and they will praise you.

Penina Tito Bazia, Sudan

238 O Lord God, this loss hurts so. My dead are so alive, I cannot believe I cannot touch them or speak to them. I so want them, Father, so miss them . . . I *bleed*, Father. Help me; help me in this fog, which blots out my perspective on the life they now live in your hereafter. Give me hope, dear Lord God, give me hope in Christ's own defeat of death, that one day I shall see my loved ones again; and touch them and hear them, not in the vividness of my mind's eye; not in dreams or memories; but in that world of light to which, O my loving Lord, safely bring me.

Ruth Etchells, England

239 O God, our heavenly Father, who does not want us, your children, to be in sorrow, come down now and be with our brothers and sisters who have lost their husbands/wives. Comfort them during their hard times, when they are alone at night or day; be with them to encourage and strengthen them. May they pass their days here on earth in the assurance that they will join you in your heavenly kingdom where there will be no more sorrow, weeping and pain.

Rhoda Ade Olarewaju, Nigeria

Man of sorrows, acquainted with grief,   240
we pray for our brothers and sisters who mourn.

We pray for each one who feels the keen grief that death can bring.
  You have told us that death is not the end of life,
  that beyond the grave is the resurrection,
  yet you wept at the side of a grave,
  you understand our grief.
  Strengthen those who mourn.

We pray for our brothers and sisters
  who are shut off from the rest of society
  by their color or their accent.
  If we are part of their trouble,
  help us to correct what lies in our power to correct.

We pray for each one who is in pain
  because of sickness or injury.
  You knew pain so deep and intense
  that you thought the heavenly Father had forgotten you.
  Be the light for those who are in the valley of the shadow.

Compassionate Savior,
  you have called us to represent you
  in compassion with your brothers and sisters who mourn.
  You have done your part;
  help us to do ours.

Andrew W Blackwood Jr, United States

241 Bless us, your waiting people, O Lord, for our focus is on you. We thank you for the comfort you give us in times of loss, grief and loneliness. Through Christ, who is the resurrection and the life, we meet each new day with courage and living hope, which lifts our burdens at the saddest moments. Your blessings, grace, love, comfort and power are enough for those suffering deep sorrows.

Lord, visit as a comforter all who are weighed down by sorrow and loneliness. Wipe away every tear from their eyes.

Peterson K Ngumo, Kenya

242   O God, in Jesus Christ you fell,
for love, into the dark earth
and died:
give us grace to wait in patient
hope and love for the rich harvest
you have promised, that will
blossom in our hearts with abundant
life and love for all the world:
through Jesus Christ we pray
who is the promise of your love
restored, renewed and multiplied.

Simon Bailey, England
(written when approaching death)

Before you, O God,   243
we remember today the ones who went before us.
Not held back by the awesomeness of the task
they followed you with tenacity and joy.
Full of courage and trust they went to new places,
ready to stand and suffer with you.

Like a cloud of many witnesses
they stand around us.

Before you, O God,
we remember the saints of our day,
who do not live by the rigid letter of the law
but by the wild demands of faith,
always prepared to give more,
always ready to be turned inside out,
knowing that new ways can only be found
through risk and pain.

Like a cloud of many witnesses
they stand around us.

Eternal God,
we thank you for the witnesses of all times and all places.
May the stories of their lives show us the richness of
   your grace.
May they inspire us to look deep within our souls.
May they encourage us to take the risk of faith
and to serve you in new ways.

Francis Brienen, United Kingdom

244   We return you to this ancient earth from which you came,
       to the broad generous plains which nurtured you
          and upon which you played and worked;
       this place wherein you found your life's work
          and made your soul's journey;
       this place whose rhythms and colours
          comforted and restored you in your sorrows;
       this place which gave you your vision
          of the one Spirit which illumines all things.

       May your spirit, released into greater freedom and light,
       bestow a blessing upon us who remain, and upon this land
          you loved.

Elizabeth Howie, Australia,
at the burial of her father

COMMUNITY

Dear people on earth, 245
I pray to you:
be my father, be my mother, be my friend.
I love you;
that's why I am born in your midst.
But I would like to tell you
that whatever happens in your communities
is your responsibility.
I'm helpless;
I'm still a child, a little one.
Help me to grow;
give me your love and care;
teach me how to be good;
and I promise you
that as an adult
I shall fully share your life, your joy,
your sorrow, your pain . . . your Dream.
I am your God, though
I am helpless.
I am waiting for you,
because you are not helpless.
I ask you this, my dear people,
in the name of love.

André Quintelier, Philippines

246

Father,
some of my friends are living
under a dark shadow of loneliness.
And loneliness is no one's friend.

Therefore, Father,
friend of the friendless,
I pray that
through me
you will become a friend

to the widow
whose loneliness is
a half-empty life,

to the adolescent
whose loneliness is
hidden in a fog of unidentity,

to the recently divorced
whose loneliness sets
him against a world of duets,

to the business leader
whose loneliness is
making decisions all alone,

to the pastor
whose loneliness is
his all-consuming love,

to the housewife
whose loneliness is
overwork without thanks.

Father,
friend of the friendless,
I pray that
you will become a friend
through me
to persons who are lonely.

Francis A Martin, United States

You have come from afar   247
and waited long and are wearied:
let us sit side by side
sharing the same bread drawn from the same source
to quiet the same hunger that makes us weak.
Then standing together
let us share the same spirit, the same thoughts
that once again draw us together in friendship and unity
    and peace.

Prières d'Ozawamick, Canadian Indian liturgical text

248

Father, Son and Holy Spirit,
One God, in perfect Community,
look now on us,
and hear our prayer for our community:
where there is falseness,
smother it by your truth;
where there is coldness,
kindle the flame of your love;
where there is joy and hope,
free us to share it together;
where there is anything
we will not do for ourselves,
make us discontent until it is done.
And make us one,
as you are one.

Before God and you who are near me,
I release anything I hold against you.
I regret all I have done to harm you.
I stand beside the wrong in my life
and ask God's forgiveness.

Before God and you who are near us,
we release anything we hold against you.
We regret all we have done to harm you.
We stand beside the wrong in our lives
and ask God's forgiveness.

The Lord Jesus Christ says to us, each one:
'Go and sin no more,
come and follow me.'
Now bind our hands with honesty
as we offer them to each other
and our prayer to you.

Iona Community, Scotland

208

The Christian life is a journey with others; 249
we travel as a people, sharing our lives,
our experiences, our hopes and fears.

Lord, with joy and in hope we welcome new travellers
to share our lives, pledging ourselves to them,
wanting to learn from and with them,
offering our experiences to them, anticipating
the form which your grace will take in them,
so that we might become the people
you want us to be.

With gratitude and pain we farewell fellow travellers
who go in answer to your call to another congregation
or who move ahead of us on the road through death.

Together we thank you for the gift of their lives
shared with us. Together we seek to support each other
in loss, to hear your word to us in bereavement,
to wait in expectation of the new beginnings
your Spirit will bring to our community.

Both in laying-hold and letting-go, we celebrate your
goodness to us, and affirm again the continuing
presence of your Spirit, blowing where you will,
forming and leading the life of your people.

Journey with us, sharing our triumphs and struggles,
and bring us safe into your eternal kingdom.

Terry C Falla, Australia

250   Almighty God,
when we see people living in accommodation
which is little better than chickens in a battery farm,
we know that you
who created humanity with the stamp of your image
cannot be satisfied.
Lord, it is true that we spoil your environment
all the time with our selfishness and sinfulness,
but we pray that you will give
architects and planners vision
and local authorities imagination
to recreate an environment
in which people will not be stifled,
but be set free to be fully the people
you always wanted them to be.
Through the love of Jesus Christ.

Eddie Neale, England

251   O God, whose nature it is to be generous:
we confess to you our share of the guilt
for a world of hungry families and homeless peoples;
forgive us for our self-centred living and spending;
forgive those who blame you for their failures.

Grant that this week some who have given nothing
may start to give;
those who have given something may give more;
that both our Church and our nation may give due place
to the cries of those who have nothing to eat
and nowhere to live;
for the sake of Jesus Christ.

Christopher Idle, England

Dear Lord, you wanted all people to live in unity and to love each 252
other. Help us to break down the walls of separation. Break down
the walls of race, colour, creed and language. Make us one so that
our unity and love for each other may win many to your fold.

Prayer of a Christian woman, Myanmar (Burma)

Lord, today you made us known to friends we did not know, 253
and you have given us seats in homes which are not our own.
You have brought the distant near,
and made a brother of a stranger,
Forgive us, Lord . . .
We did not introduce you.

Unknown, Polynesia

God of mystery, 254
draw us nearer to you.
God of relationship,
draw us nearer to each other.
God in Trinity,
draw us into deeper understanding
through your gift of faith
and the outpouring of your love.

Joy Tetley, England

255   In the face of all our realities:
        we are the people who heal each other,
        who grow strong together,
        who name the truth,
        who know what it means
        to live in community,
        moving towards a common dream
        for a new heaven and a new earth
        in the power of the love of God,
        the company of Jesus Christ
        and the leading of the Holy Spirit.

The people of Pitt Street Uniting Church, Sydney, Australia

JUSTICE, FREEDOM, PEACE

JUSTICE

God, many times we come to you in prayer. Over and over again 256
we ask you to show us how to live, how to be just, how to love,
how to be faithful. Today we come again.

God, we are a people who long to see your face. Sometimes, you
seem very far away. We begin to doubt. We become discouraged.

Often, our own actions or the actions of the communities to which
we belong, deny our prayers. It is easy to say 'Lord, Lord . . .'. It is
much harder to take responsibility for what needs to be done.
Sometimes in our prayers we wish to keep you in church and not
in every part of our lives. Sometimes, we prefer pious practices
rather than commitment to the works of justice.

God, help us not to turn our face from human need. Open our eyes
to what we can do personally, what we can do as a community, and
to what changes need to be made so that justice is available to
everyone.

Women's World Day of Prayer, 1990

As you anointed kings and called prophets of old, lead us to recognize 257
our true representatives and authentic leaders: men and women
   who love your people and can walk with them;
   who feel their pain and share their joys;
   who dream their dreams;
   and strive to accompany them to their common goal.
In your fire – with your Spirit –
   embolden and commission us
   to transform our political system,
   to serve your people
   and to bring real glory to your name.

Unknown, Philippines

258   You, African woman, yes, you
       with your ebony black complexion;
       You African woman
       the mother of a wonderful continent:

       Like any other woman in the world
       you have lived in ignorance,
       you have lived amid untold sufferings,
       you have known submission,
       you have known humiliation,
       you have known slavery
       and you have sought your freedom.

       Rejoice, for you have been heard,
       you, with your black ebony complexion;
       God has heard your cry and lifted up his countenance
           upon you.

       O African woman,
       shed the yoke you have been bearing
       from the beginning of time;
       put on again the dignity by which God created you
       in His image and stand proud – proud to be a woman,
       the mother of the black continent.
       Like any other woman in the world, perform your role
       as a woman giving life through her blood;
       fulfil your destiny, you African woman,
       in dignity, justice and peace.

                         Rachel James Moukoko, Iona Community

O God, help us to work for justice   259
for the indigenous people of this land,
suffering from white settlement
and the dominance of European culture.
Give us the faith and courage
to accept this responsibility.

O God, recreate relationships
between women and men
and give us a sense of hope.
Give us gentleness in our strength
and courage in claiming our lives.

O God, renew the lives
of those who are victims of crime
that they may recover a sense of safety and trust.
May the elderly be free of fear,
the poor be given new power
and the rich learn compassion and generosity.

O God, give us open arms
for those who flee from violences around the world:
the wars, the tortures and the imprisonments.
May the refugees who come to us for sanctuary
be warmed and encouraged in hope.

O God, help us to preserve freedom
when we ask for security,
compassion and equity when we demand justice.
Give us respect for those who are different
and openness to those who model new possibilities.

O God, in this complex world,
we need your strength and your power to give us hope,
your courage to keep faith in the future of humanity.

The people of Pitt Street Uniting Church, Sydney, Australia

260   Our Father, who are in this our land,
    may your name be blessed
    in our incessant search for justice and peace.
    May your kingdom come
    for those who have for centuries awaited a life with dignity.
    May your will be done on earth and in heaven
    and in the Church of Central America,
    a Church on the side of the poor.
    Give us today our daily bread to build a new society.
    Forgive us our trespasses,
    do not let us fall into the temptation
    of believing ourselves already new men and women.
    And deliver us from the evil of war
    and from the evil of forgetting that our lives
    and the life of this country are in your hands.

The Lord's Prayer as used by Christian communities in Nicaragua

261 Lord, in these times when we are about to lose hope and our efforts seem futile, grant that we may perceive in our hearts and minds the image of your resurrection which remains our only source of courage and strength, so that we may continue to face the challenges, and struggle against hardship and oppression born of injustice.

People from a slum area, Philippines

O God, as a black man, I get exceedingly tired and so filled up with   262
confronting and fighting racism, that formidable foe. It passes its
poison from one generation to another. It has polluted all of the
wellsprings of the nation's institutional life. More widespread than
the drug scourge, more explosive than nuclear weapons, more crip-
pling than germ warfare – racism has washed up on the shores of
every nation of every continent.

O God, I get tired of racism wherever I go – abroad and at home.
From stores that let me know I have gotten 'out of place'; from
looks of fear that my black manly presence engenders in some; from
small insults to major offenses; from polite, subtle, condescending
paternalism or maternalism to outright, open hostility; from insult-
ing jokes about my intelligence to curiosity about alleged black
sexual prowess; from caricatures and stereotypes to the 'you are the
exception' syndrome – racism rears its many heads and shows its
various faces all the time.

Yet as I bow before you, O God, I pledge to you, to my ancestors who sacrificed greatly so that I might enjoy whatever rights
and privileges – however limited or circumscribed – are mine to
experience, and to my children and to their children that I will keep
up the noble fight of faith and perseverance. I will not go back to
the back of the bus. I will not accept the invincibility of racism and
the inviolability of its mythical sacred precepts.

I know that greater is the One that is in me than the one that is
in the world. May that Spirit's presence and power direct and
inspire me now and evermore until victory is won for my people,
and all people, and until the kingdoms of this world become the
kingdom of our Lord and of his Christ.

William Donnel Watley, United States

263   God of life,
we pray to you for all people:

for all women who have been excluded from a full-fledged
life for the only reason that it has been always like that.
Empower us to take all iniquity away.

for all people who are oppressed and abused.
Empower us to take all iniquity away.

for all people whose freedom and dignity are denied by
systems and authorities.
Empower us to take all iniquity away.

for all those who are driven away from their houses and their
homes because of their conscience and their convictions.
Empower us to take all iniquity away.

for all those who are in search of the meaning of their life
within their own culture and religion.
Empower us to take all iniquity away.

for all those who have to labour too hard for too small a salary.
Empower us to take all iniquity away.

for all those who – from sheer necessity – have to sell their
own body.
Empower us to take all iniquity away.

for those many desperate women and men who are at the
mercy of the rich and the powerful.
Empower us to take all iniquity away.

for all those who suffer, we pray to you.
Empower us to take all iniquity away.

André Quintelier, Philippines

O God, may your Church discover, then identify, its life with 264
groups of people who suffer injustice and remain unheard. May
your Church be the voice of the voiceless. Let your Church find
them, and struggle with them, and so find the way of your cross,
and the way to true responsibility.

Emilio Castro, Uruguay

From the land of the Resurrection and the cradle of the promise of 265
salvation to all humankind through Jesus Christ our Lord, and with
a candle of hope, we pray to you, God our Father, that the action
of peace-seekers and peace-makers may bear fruit so that
> hope will take the place of despair,
> justice will prevail over oppression,
> peace will turn strife into love.

Palestinian women, Jerusalem

Justice, justice is what is needed, O God, in the Sudan, in Africa and 266
in the world.
> God, you hate what is evil, you love what is right.
> God the Father, God the Son, God the Holy Spirit, when justice
is done, the righteous rejoice. But it brings terror to evildoers.
> Sudan, Africa and the world need justice, not terror. It is only
you, O God, who can bring justice.
> O Father, Son and Holy Spirit, when there is justice, there is
peace, in Sudan, in Africa, in the world.
> We cry for justice in the name of our Elder Brother, Jesus Christ.

Ezekiel Kondo, Sudan

267 O Christ, you are the light of the world (*light candle*). Shine into
the dark places and expose the sins of greed, oppression, hate and
violence. Fill us with love, joy, peace, patience and a willingness to
forgive.

O Christ, you are the light of the world (*light candle*). We pray for
the homeless, the refugees, the expelled and forgotten people
everywhere. Strengthen us in our belief that you are a God of justice. Empower us with the determination to work for basic human
rights.

O Christ, you are the light of the world (*light candle*). We pray for
people everywhere and in particular for the people of the Middle
East. Show us how we are to live together as neighbours, understanding and respecting one another. We remember before you the
many places in the world where there is conflict between nations.
We pray that love may determine a just solution.

O Christ, you are the light of the world (*light candle*). As the Risen
Christ you broke the chains of death; free us from every kind of
oppression. Breathe your Holy Spirit upon us. Make us a people
of hope, who live in lands where there is peace and justice for
everyone.

Women's World Day of Prayer, 1994,
written by women from Jerusalem

Almighty and everlasting King, Prince of peace, Creator of the 268
heavens and the earth in a righteous order, you are our heavenly
father who rules us with all your justice. We offer our prayer of
thanksgiving.

We acknowledge that we have lived unjustly with one another
and within your creation.

You intended us to live in straightness. You expected honest living,
that we would treat others justly and fairly, for life's highest reality
is being just and doing God's will. How can we be just before you
our God?

We have embraced violence. We have not been righteous. Have
mercy on us.

We plead that the world's morality may measure up to your
standard of justice. May men, women, young people and children
seek to do justice.

There are national governments which we trust are ordained by
you, Lord. We plead for the leaders that they may act justly with
your people. As they deliberate, God help them always to have a
mind that is in Christ Jesus, to make righteous resolutions and rec-
ommendations. Governments are supposed to be advocating right
and fair living, but instead they advocate murder, corruption,
depriving people of social rights, poor education systems, economic
decline, misappropriation of funds, poor health facilities, slums,
poor road conditions, war. Lord, help world leaders to understand
that your righteousness is a consuming fire.

Lord, we need someone to understand. Grant unto us justice that
we may praise you.

R Gicharu, Kenya

269   We are here, Lord, because we believe.
        It is your gift and our struggle.
        Help us to free ourselves from all that enslaves us.

        Lord, set me free.

        We are here, Lord, because we believe in justice.
        It is your gift and our struggle.
        Help us to work for justice in our own lives
        in our nation and in the world.

        God of justice, lead us on.

        We are here, Lord, because we believe in unity.
        It is your gift and our struggle.
        Help us to build bridges, to reach out
        in solidarity, in sisterhood and brotherhood.

        Lord, make us one.

        We are here, Lord, because we believe in peace.
        It is your gift and our struggle.
        Help us change the injustices and inequalities
        that destroy true peace.

        God, of peace, lead us on.

                            from an Action for World Development service
                                    held in Brisbane, Australia

FREEDOM

As we closed our doors this morning, and walked freely through the   270
church door, other doors slammed behind other people, and they
do not know if or when they will open again: doors in prison cells
and torture chambers; doors separating families, doors in labour
camp units. Let us ask Christ, who came to set all men free, to
enable us to experience his freedom and to bring that freedom to
others.

Pax Christi, international Roman Catholic peace organisation

O Lord Jesus,   271
please abide with me.
Dispel my deep loneliness!
No one can be my companion for ever,
but you are the Lord who is everywhere,
present at all times.
Only you are my dear companion and saviour.

In the long dark night,
along the silent shadowy pathways,
I beg you to grasp my hand.
When others have forgotten me,
please remember me in eternity!
In the name of Jesus.

Dr Andrew Song, China
(a theologian who spent many years in prison)

272   I call on you, Lord, in a time of persecution.
Hear me, God of justice,
deliver me from my enemies.
I have been labelled a subversive, and arrested by the military,
torn from among my people, to the terror of the village,
of women and children terrified by the violence of cowardly
    men.
I have disappeared with those who are called terrorists,
in a headspinning journey,
full of threats and humiliations, blows and questions,
thrown among prisoners.
In secrecy and isolation,
far from my people and my friends,
lost in time and space,
I am abandoned to an unknown fate.

I was a caricature of a man,
my eyes blindfolded,
my clothing torn,
subject to mockery and oaths,
defenceless and vulnerable.
I was a target, exposed to treacherous blows.
From the first moment,
they pulled the trigger of their sub-machine gun
to simulate an execution,
to make me confess to crimes
invented by my enemies.

Robbed of all my dignity,
with death for close companion,
in these hours of trial, Lord,
I was not alone.
I knew your presence, you who are my strength,
you who are my hope,
you who are my deliverer.

Psalm of an unknown Brazilian prisoner

Jesus, who was lost and found in the garden,   273
never to be lost again,
stand by us in the darkness of our crucifixions,
as the women stood by you.
Die and rise with us in the suffering of the world.
Be reborn with us
as love and hope and faith and endurance
outlast cruelty and death.

Kathy Keay, England

274 So many years of wailing winds and bitter rain,
so many years of violent storms.
Unseen in the tempest is the courtyard of the Lord,
shed on the sacrificial altar is the fresh blood of Abraham.
Where are you, vine of God?
Where are you, fragrant pine tree of God?
Where are you? Where are you?

Every lamb is crying out, every lost sheep is sorrowing.
The sheep of Jehovah are astray on the steppes,
the tears of the distressed are shed in the west wind.
Where are you, good Shepherd?
Where are you, good Protector?
Where are you? Where are you?

Jerusalem in my dreams, Jerusalem in my tears.
I have sought you in the fire of the sacrificial altar.
I have sought you in the nail holes of the Cross.
How long before I can leave the Valley of Tears?
How long before I can return to home in paradise?
How long? How long?

Simon Zhao, China, on finding no Christian fellowship
after release from prison

Lord Jesus, 275
you experienced in person
the sufferings and the death of a prisoner of conscience.
You were plotted against, betrayed by a friend,
and arrested under cover of darkness
by men who came with clubs and swords.
You were tortured, beaten and humiliated,
and sentenced to an agonising death
though you had done no wrong.
Be now with prisoners of conscience throughout the world.
Be with them in the darkness of the dungeon,
in the loneliness of separation from those they love;
be with them in their fear of what may come to them,
in the agony of their torture
and in the face of execution and death.
Stretch out your hands in power
to break their chains and to open the gates of freedom,
so that your kingdom of justice
may be established now among them.

Michael Evans, England

God of mercy and hope, 276
in the struggle for freedom grant us strength;
in decisions about freedom grant us wisdom;
in the practice of freedom grant us guidance;
in the dangers of freedom grant us protection;
in the life of freedom grant us joy
and in the use of freedom grant us vision;
for your name's sake.

Latin American Council of Churches

277   Father!
Your Spirit told us
through the mouth of Paul
that the whole earth
and we too
as your children
groan
in the pains of a birth!
It is easy, Lord,
to grasp and affirm this.
For there are passages
so difficult
and hours
so filled with anguish
that the image really applies:
they are labour pains!
Something is being born.
Who knows?
    A world in which men and women can breathe,
    a more just, a more human world!

Dom Helder Camara, Brazil

God, our promised land; 278
Christ, our way,
our journey has become long and hard
because we wander about
like nomads
not knowing where to go.
We are strangers in our own land,
without bread, a roof, a future.
But you came to find us
with your life-giving breath.
You, who are also displaced,
have become an exile with us.
You offer us anew the promised land.
Your spirit urges us toward
that joyous homecoming.

Displaced people, Peru

Lord God, Creator and Saviour of mankind, please hear the earnest 279
entreaties of your Chinese sons and daughters. Your Holy Son
offered his life to save the world, to free people from sin and evil so
we can regain freedom. We earnestly beseech you to use the power
of the Holy Spirit to free the Chinese people from danger and
hardship, that the whole nation from top to bottom may deal with
the present situation in a peaceful and intelligent manner. May we
at an early date realize democracy, the rule of law and respect for
human rights.

Compassionate God, please fill us with the strength of will to
bear the hardships of the nation, and to be faithful to the nation and
the people. We firmly believe that you are the source of justice and
power. You are eternal life and the eternal King.

Roman Catholic Christians in China,
after the massacre in Tiananmen Square

PEACE

280 Father Almighty, we pray for your peace on earth.

      For peace that is life-giving;
      for peace that is love-bearing;
      for peace that is true freedom;
      for peace that is purposeful;
      for peace that is prevailing.

      Father, we pray for children in time of war; they are so defenceless.

      We pray for the old; they are unable to escape danger quickly.

      We pray for those with physical disabilities; they are at the mercy of others.

      We pray for women; they are so vulnerable to abuse.

      We pray for the innocent; they suffer for the unjust desires of others.

      We pray for those whose lives will be changed by war:
      those who are blinded;
      those who are burned;
      those who lose limbs;
      those who lose their reason;
      those who lose their peace of mind;
      those who lose their health and strength for ever.

      Father, above all we pray for those in anguish; those whose lives will never be the same again; those who have lost their loved ones; those who have lost their lives.

      Father, deepen our desire for peace; restore our resolve for peace; increase our intent to work for peace.

      Will for us your peace, perfect and prevailing, for your Son, our Saviour Christ's sake.

Pamela Wilding, Kenya

Give us courage, Lord, to stand up and be counted, 281
to stand up for those who cannot stand up for themselves,
to stand up for ourselves when it is needful for us to do so.
Let us fear nothing more than we fear you,
let us love nothing more than we love you,
for thus we shall fear nothing also.
Let us have no other God before you,
whether nation or party or state or church.
Let us seek no other peace
but the peace which is yours,
and make us its instruments,
opening our eyes and our ears and our hearts,
so that we should know always
what work of peace we may do for you.

Alan Paton, South Africa

Our need, please God, is true peace in the world. 282
Peace of mind,
yes, that's what everyone prays for.

What is our state in the world?
Come and see how our people are destroying the world,
without seeking what is in your heart,
without seeking what is in your mind.

Yes, if we seek peace,
God will grant us peace.
It is peace
that encourages our heart;
and making peace
that is the guarantee of hope.

Ikoli Harcourt Whyte, Nigeria

283   Our globe is nothing but a little star in the great universe.
It is our duty to turn this globe into a planet
whose creatures are not tormented by wars,
nor tortured by hunger and fear,
nor torn apart in senseless divisions
according to race, colour or creed.
Give us the courage and foresight, to begin this work
    even today,
so that our children and grandchildren may one day
    take pride
in being called human.

Stephen Vincent Benet, United States
(this is the prayer of the United Nations)

284 O God, save our shores from the weapons of death, our lands from the things that deny our young ones love and freedom. Let the seas of the Pacific Ocean carry messages of peace and goodwill. Turn away from our midst any unkind and brutal practices. Let each child swim and breathe the fresh air that is filled by the Holy Spirit.

    O Lord Jesus, bless all who are makers of that inner peace that breaks down the barriers of hatred, and unite us with the open arms of your cross, that all the peoples of the world may live happily together.

Amanuka Havea, Tonga

O living God, God of all the earth,   285
send down the Spirit of your Son Jesus Christ;
heal our wounded hearts;
make peace in the place of conflict;
grant love in the face of revenge;
build hope where fear prevailed;
establish trust across our divisions.
Let the light of truth disperse the shadows,
and the dawn of justice banish hatred,
that our lives may be saved,
our land restored,
Africa set free
and the love of God be known in joy for all.

Bishop Peter Lee, South Africa;
this is known as the Sharpeville Prayer

We believe that as Christians we are called to be peace-makers, in 286
the true peace which God promises us.

We believe that this may sometimes mean 'disturbing the peace' as
Jesus did, for a purpose – to restore the purpose of God.

We believe that our Pacific ways are also a gift from God; we are
invited to use the values of our Pacific culture to build societies of
justice and peace.

We express these beliefs, reminded of the love of God, the grace of
Christ, and the fellowship of the Holy Spirit.

Women of the Pacific

287   Father of mercies,
        open our spirits and our hearts
        so that we may be more truly makers of peace.
        Remember all those who are oppressed,
        who suffer and die.
        May your kingdom of justice, peace and love
        come for all men of every race and tongue,
        and may all the earth be filled with your glory.

adapted from a prayer by Pope Paul VI

288   Let us pray for those who foster violence,
        those who do not forgive others.
        May the Lord change their hearts
        that they seek peace and love their brothers and sisters.

Unknown, Ivory Coast

289   To you, Creator of nature and humanity,
        of truth and beauty, I pray:
        Hear my voice, for it is the voice of the victim of all wars
        and violence among individuals and nations.
        Hear my voice, for it is the voice of all children who suffer
        and will suffer when people put their faith in weapons and war.
        Hear my voice when I beg you to instil into the hearts of all
        human beings the wisdom of peace, the strength of justice,
        and the joy of fellowship.
        O God, hear my voice, and grant unto the world your
          everlasting peace.

Pope John Paul II

BLESSINGS

Glory be to you, O Holy God, you who are love and justice. 290
We praise you for the gifts you have made in creating the world
   and human beings in your likeness.
We praise you for opening up for us a new way of life in
   Jesus Christ.
We praise you for calling us, through the Holy Spirit, to follow
   Jesus Christ and to seek to bring justice to all.

Women's World Day of Prayer, 1990

And now to him who is able to keep us from falling, and lift us from 291
the dark valley of despair to the bright mountain of hope, from the
midnight of desperation to the daybreak of joy; to him be power
and authority, for ever and ever.

Martin Luther King Jr, United States

May the God who shakes heaven and earth, 292
   whom death could not contain,
   who lives to disturb and heal us,
   bless you with power to go forth
   and proclaim the Gospel.

Janet Morley, England

293   Start your walk towards the place where God wants you.
        May God enlarge your sleeping mat; may God enlarge
            the door of your dwelling; may God enlarge your back.
        May God lead you by pulling you along, and may God
            push you.
        May God be at your side.
        May God grant you many children.
        May God grant you many cattle.
        Spread out, like the water of a lake. May God be your
            deliverer.
        I have placed myself in front of you to lead you.

        Start your walk towards the place where God wants you.
        May God enlarge everything that is yours.
        Be like a powerful tree, with a refreshing shadow.
        Give us life.
        Go without stopping.
                                            Samburu people, Kenya

294 My God, place me where I may be held tightly by you. O God, let
me become like a liana, like millet with very many small grains.
God of the mountain of my ancestors, hear me!

    May God be favourable to you: be vigorous like a tree that lasts
through the annual blossoming of its shoots.

    My God, grant me light for my eyes to see all things.

    My God, you who are here and elsewhere, be a God who sees
and hears. And God said, 'All right!'
                                            Samburu people, Kenya

244

O God, you have let me pass this day in peace,   295
let me pass the night in peace.
O Lord who has no Lord,
there is no strength but in you.
You alone have no obligation.
Under your hand I pass the night.
You are my mother and my father.

Boran people, Kenya

May you be for us a moon of joy and happiness. Let the young 296
become strong and the grown man maintain his strength, the pregnant woman be delivered and the woman who has given birth
suckle her child. Let the stranger come to the end of his journey
and those who remain at home dwell safely in their houses. Let the
flocks that go to feed in the pastures return happily. May you be a
moon of harvest and of calves. May you be a moon of restoration
and of good health.

Mensa people, Ethiopia

May God stride out before you on your journey   297
through life
and through prayer.

May Jesus, your playful brother,
pace you in his holy way to the end.

May the Holy Spirit greet you at
each corner and cuddle you to her breast.

Siân Swain Taylor, Wales

245

298 Lord of Light – shine on us,
Lord of Peace – dwell in us,
Lord of Might – succour us,
Lord of Love – enfold us,
Lord of Wisdom – enlighten us.
Then, Lord, let us go out as your witness, in obedience to your
command; to share the Good News of your love for us in the gift
of your Son, our Saviour, Jesus Christ.

St Asaph Mothers' Union, Wales

299   God the Sender, send us,
God the Sent, come with us,
God the Strengthener of those who go, empower us,
that we may go with you
and find those who will call you
Father, Son and Holy Spirit.

Church in Wales

O Creator and Mighty God,   300
you have promised
   strength for the weak,
   rest for the labourers,
   light for the way,
   grace for the trials,
   help from above,
   unfailing sympathy,
   undying love.
O Creator and Mighty God,
help us to continue in your promise.

Unknown, Pakistan

INDEX OF FIRST LINES

May this Eucharist, conquering doubt and fear 26

May you be for us a moon of joy and happiness 296

May your blessing rest on the new home 201

Most heavenly Father of the human race, behold me 223

Most loving God, you are the Shepherd God 110

My God, have mercy on our children 209

My God, I need to have signs of your grace 32

My God, place me where I may be held tightly by you 294

Nailed to a cross because you would not compromise 52

Now I am old, Lord 233

O Christ, as we walk through the land that you loved 53

O Christ, you are the light of the world 267

O Christ, you are united to every human being without exception 56

O Creator and Mighty God 300

O God, as a black man, I get exceedingly tired 262

O God, by your providence the blood of the martyrs is the seed 97

O God, enlarge my heart 126

O God Eternal, good beyond all that is good 134

O God, help us to work for justice 259

O God, I don't find much contentment in my job 212

O God, in Jesus Christ you fell 242

O God, may your Church discover 264

O God, only you know the truth of the burden 190

O God, our Father, Creator of the universe 45

O God our Father, I thank you for giving me health and strength 31

O God, our Father, the fountain of love, power and justice 124

O God our heavenly Father, as we light this candle 68

O God, our heavenly Father, who does not want us, your children, to be in sorrow 239

O God, save our shores from the weapons of death 284

O God, slow us down 168

O God, Sustainer of all life 102

O God, the giver of life 137

O God, we have come together in prayer 17

O God, we remember not only our son but also his murderers 235

O God, who by a star guided the wise men 44

O God who travels with us in the shadows 93

O God, whose nature it is to be generous 251

O God, whose will it is that all your children should be one 136

O God, you have let me pass this day in peace 295

O God, you have prepared in peace the path I must follow today 163

O God, you took your Son from our midst 128

O Holy Spirit of God, help us to realise 112

O Jesus, be the canoe that holds me up in the sea of life 167

O Jesus Christ, you knew the workshop of Joseph 216

O living God, God of all the earth 285

O Lord, be gracious unto us 186

O Lord God, our Father. You are the light that can never be put out 59

O Lord God, this loss hurts so 238

O Lord, I felt such terrible disappointment and sadness 236

INDEX OF COUNTRIES

Some regions and continents are included alongside countries

255

256

INDEX OF AUTHORS

Churches and Christian groups are included alongside individuals

INDEX OF SUBJECTS

see also forgiveness
redemption *see* salvation
refugees 40, 42, 193, 259, 263, 267, 278
rejection 193 *see also* abandonment
relaxation 166
religiosity 20, 64, 182, 256
renewal 19, 33, 47, 50, 67, 73, 75, 119,
    143, 162, 187, 221 *see also* church
    renewal; new life
respect 200, 259
responsibility 125
resurrection 52 *see also* Easter; Jesus
    Christ, resurrection
revival *see* renewal
riches *see* wealth
righteousness 24, 70, 268 *see also* justice
rural life 84

sacraments 32 *see also* baptism; eucharist
sacrifice 173
sadness 34, 198, 239, 241
safety *see* security
saints 98, 243
salvation 22, 37, 43, 53, 177, 198, 285 *see
    also* God's forgiveness and mercy
scripture *see* Bible; word of God
security 153, 180, 198, 211, 259
self-awareness 102, 171, 189
self-deceit 20
self-importance 164
self-indulgence 20
self-sacrifice 100
selfishness 48, 62, 87, 153, 181, 183, 251
service of God 16–18, 73, 91, 121, 200,
    222, 243 *see also* God's will,
    dedication to
sharing 28, 30, 33, 57, 83, 127, 140, 185,
    190 *see also* social justice
Sharpeville Prayer 285
sickness 20, 147, 164, 222, 231, 240, 280
    see also healing; health
Simeon 37
slavery 173, 182
social justice 12, 19, 33–4, 133, 185,
    214–15, 277 *see also* sharing

social workers 226
solitude *see* loneliness
sorrow *see* sadness
South Africa 12
space exploration 108
spells 80
spirits 123
stewardship *see* creation, reverence for
street children 193 *see also* homelessness
strength 16, 18–19, 22, 31, 75, 130, 150,
    168, 220, 255, 261, 276, 289 *see also*
    God's comfort and strength; God's
    power; weakness
strong, the 105 *see also* power
success 133, 164
Sudan 266
suffering 20, 34, 96, 107, 124, 164, 175,
    258, 263, 275, 287
sympathy 94

temptation 62
thankfulness 7–8, 16, 59, 70, 161, 193 *see
    also* gratitude
theologians 138
time 161, 213 *see also* future, the; past,
    the;
torture 270, 275
tranquillity 220 *see also* peace
travellers 40
troubles 178, 190
trust 57, 66, 70, 114, 150, 160, 165–6,
    169, 180, 198, 243, 285; in God 17,
    138, 153, 206, 227, 235, 273, 291 *see
    also* faith
truth 19, 22, 32–3, 60, 70, 93, 100, 207,
    248, 285 *see also* honesty

Uganda, martyrs of 97
underprivileged, the 133 *see also* social
    justice
understanding *see* wisdom and
    understanding
unemployment *see* employment
unfairness 178
unforgiving, the 288 *see also* forgiveness

270

ACKNOWLEDGEMENTS

Twenty-four prayers were written especially for this volume and submitted by colleges, institutes, churches and university faculties in relationship with SPCK Worldwide. They came from Jamaica   113, 216; Kenya   60, 62, 71, 106, 109, 111, 122, 193, 198, 241, 268, 280; Nigeria   101, 197; South Africa 47, 285; Sudan   266; Tanzania   18; Uganda   154; and Zimbabwe   77, 102, 200. Copyright in these prayers is with SPCK.

Permission to use the following prayers has been kindly granted by the copyright holders. We made our best endeavour to track all sources, but if we are told of any errors, these will be corrected at reprint.

Anglican Consultative Council   45, 67, 75, 114, 116, 117, 118, 119, 120, 121, 123, 184, 299, 300

Appleton, George, quoted from Jim Cotter *Prayers at Night*   224

Augsburg Fortress Press, 426 South Fifth Street, Box 1209, Minneapolis, MN 55440-1209, © 1974 Leslie F. Brandt, *A Book of Christian Prayer*   128, 212, 229

Baker Book House Co, Box 6287, Grand Rapids, Michigan 49516-6287, © 1969 Andrew W. Blackwood Jr, *Prayers from the City*   217, 240

Bantam, Doubleday, Dell Publishing Group, 1540 Broadway, New York 10036, © 1996 Desmond Tutu, *An African Prayer Book*, UK Edition Hodder & Stoughton, a division of Hodder Headline, 338 Euston Road, London NW1 3BH   10, 25, 145, 163, 296

Brethren Press, 1451 Dundee Avenue, Elgin, Illinois 60120, © 1979 Mary Sue H. Rosenberger, *Sacraments in a Refrigerator*   40, 208, 230

HarperCollins, 77-85 Fulham Palace Road, London W6 8JB, © 1985, compiled by Anthony Gittings CSSP, *The Heart of Prayer* 3, 9, 153, 80, 209, 293, 294, 295

HarperCollins, London, © 1994, Kathy Keay, *Laughter, Silence and Shouting* 258, 273, 292

HarperCollins, 10 East 53rd Street, New York 10022, © 1994 James Melvin Washington (compiler), *Conversations with God* 168, 246, 262; D. J. Fleming (compiler), *The World at One in Prayer* 91

Hengrave Community of Reconciliation 139

Indian National Industrial Mission 33

Irish School of Ecumenics, Dublin, newsletter 'Unity' 194

Joint Board of Christian Education Melbourne, edited 1996 Noel Nicholls and Philip Liebelt, *Gentle Rain on Parched Earth* 219, 244

Jubilate Hymns, 61 Chessel Avenue, Southampton SO19 4DY, quoted from © 1995 HarperCollins, London, *World Praise* 19, 35

Latin America Press 256

Lion Publishing, Peters Way, Sandy Lane West, Oxford, OX4 5HG, © Maureen Edwards, *Pray With Us* 41, 178, 214

McCrimmons, 10-12 High Street, Great Wakering, Essex SS3 0EQ, © 1972/73 Michael Hollings and Eta Gullick, *It's Me, Lord* 133, 150, 196

Mambo Press, Gweru, Zimbabwe, © 1981 *The Gospel according to the Ghetto* 127

Maraschin, Jaci C. © 1987 129

Mayhew, Kevin, Rattlesden, Bury St Edmunds, Suffolk IP30 0SZ, © 1979 Michael Evans (compiler), *Let My People Go* 12, 270, 275

Methodist Church (UK) Prayer Handbook 1993/94 276

Mothers' Union, Mary Sumner House, 24 Tufton Street, London SW1P 3RB, © 1994, HarperCollins/Marshall Pickering, Rachel Stowe (compiler), *Women at Prayer* 16, 31, 38, 68, 135, 167, 181, 197, 199, 204, 205, 207, 211, 223, 236, 237, 239, 298

Mowbray, Villiers House, 41/47 Strand, London WC2N 5JE, © 1991 Alan Hunter (compiler), *Prayers and Thoughts of Chinese Christians* 271, 274, 279

Neue Stadt Verlag, Munich, translated from © Citta Nuova Editrice Rome, Chiara Lubich, *Spiel mi göttlichen Rollen* 175

Newman Press, 1865 Broadway, New York 10023, © 1973 Missionary Society of Paul the Apostle in the State of New York, Pierre Talec translated by Edmond Bonin, *Bread in the Desert*, originating publisher © 1971 Centurion/le Cerf, Paris 26, 27, 35, 39, 51, 58, 177

Open Book Publishers, 205 Halifax Street, Adelaide, South Australia 5000, © 1981 Terry Falla, *Be Our Freedom, Lord* 5, 249; © 1979 Bruce D. Prewer, *Australian Psalms* 24, 54, 65; © 1983 Bruce D. Prewer, *Australian Prayers* 11, 63, 110, 156

Orbis Books, PO Box 308, Maryknoll, New York 10545-0308, Helder Camara, *Hoping Against All Hope*, originating publisher Pendo Verlag, Zurich 148, 277; *The Desert Is Fertile*, originating publisher Desclee de Brewer, Paris 172

Osservatore Romano, © 1994 Ecumenical Patriarch Bartholomew, *Via Crucis* 46

Patmos Verlag, Dusseldorf, Germany, © 1987, Christel Voss-Goldstein (compiler), *Abel, Wo Ist Deine Schwester?* 233

Paulist Press, 997 MacArthur Blvd, Mahwah, NJ 07430, © Huub Oosterhuis, *Your Word Is Near* 104

Philippines, National Christian Council of the, © 1989 *What Does the Lord Require of Us?* 179

Presbyterian Church in Cameroon 81

Robertson, Josephine, *Prayers for the Later Years* 232, 234

Seremane, Joe (permission sought) quoted © 1996 International Bible Reading Association *Living Prayers for Today* compiled by Maureen Edwards 187

Seuil, Editions du, France, © 1957 Teilhard de Chardin, *Le Milieu Divin* 231

South India, Church of 44, 115, 188

SPCK/Triangle, Holy Trinity Church, Marylebone Road, London NW1 4DU, © 94 Ruth Etchells, *Just As I Am* 48, 64, 201, 238; © 1997 Josephine Bax, *Help on the Way* 202; © 1986 John Carden, *Another Day*, from which are quoted: Church Missionary Society, London, Subir Biswas, *Lord Let Me Share* 78, 92; Darton, Longman and Todd, London, Michael Bordeaux, *Risen Indeed* 149, and Helder Camara, *A Thousand Reasons for Living* 29; William Heinemann, Oxford, Alfonso M. di Nola, *The Prayers of Man* 85; Orbis Books, Maryknoll, New York, Walter Buhlman, *The Coming of the Third Church* 98; Peter Pauper Press, New York 186; United Church of Pakistan, *Lahore Diocesan Leaflet* 152; 6th WCC World Assembly, Vancouver 1983, *Jesus Christ Light of the World* 30, 140; Exact source unknown 144, 253; © 1992 Christian Aid (co-publication) edited Janet Morley, *Bread of Tomorrow*, in which are quoted: 1987 British Council of Churches, *All Year Round* 282; 1987 Latin America Press, *Paginas* 83, 278; 1990 Asian Institute for Liturgy and Music, *Sound the Bamboo* (prayer paraphrased by James Minchin) 169; 1988 British Council of Churches, *All Year Round* 273; 1989 Wild Goose Worship Group, *A Wee Worship Book* 2, 160; 1974 Sheed and Ward, Helder Camara, *The Desert Is Fertile* 82; 1986 Bible Reading Fellowship *Our World God's World* edited Barbara Wood 88; exact source unknown 89; © 1987 compiled Robert Runcie and Basil Hume, *Prayers for Peace* 287, 289; © 1995 Catherine von Ruhland, *Prayers from the Edge* 225, 227, 228, 242; © 1995 *SPCK Book of Christian Prayer* 45, 50, 59, 105, 136, 281, 291; H. Deqhani-Tafti, *The Hard Awakening* 235; Kathy Galloway, *Love Burning Deep* 166; Mother Teresa edited by Kathryn Spink, *In the Shadow of the Heart* 222; Oliver Davies ed., *Celtic Christian Spirituality* 297

Sunday Visitor Inc, 200 Noll Plaza, Huntington, Indiana 46750, © 1974 written and compiled by Robert J. Fox, *A Catholic Prayer Book* 174

Taizé, Ateliers et Presses de, Prayers by Brother Roger of Taizé, 71250 Taizé Community, France 1, 56, 61, 66, 76, 132, 146, 151, 159, 165

Tetley, Joy   20, 43, 49, 55, 99, 170, 221, 254

Thompson, Ken, © 1976, *Bless This Desk*   210, 213, 220

Uganda, Anglican Church of, Kampala   97

United Church of Christ Board for World Ministries, United States, Calendar of Prayer 1986–87   155

United Nations, New York   283

United Reformed Church, 86 Tavistock Place, London WC1H 9RT, 1995 *A Restless Hope*, © Francis Brienen   7, 57, 90, 161, 243; © Bernard Thorogood   107, 158; © 1997, *Reigndance*   15

Uniting Church in Australia, Sydney, *We Believe*   79

Uniting Education, PO Box 1245, Collingwood, 3066, Australia, © 1993 Dorothy McCrae-McMahon, *The Glory of Blood, Sweat and Tears*   28, 95, 190; © 96 Dorothy McCrae-McMahon, *Echoes of our Journey*   4, 69, 93, 255, 259

Uzima Press, St Johns Gate, Irwin House, PO Box 48127, Nairobi, © William N. Richards and James Richardson, *Prayers for Today*   73, 84, 87, 100, 203, 215, 218

Wild Goose Publications, *Iona Worship Book*   248

Women's World Day of Prayer, Commercial Road, Tunbridge Wells, Kent, TN1 2RR   8, 17, 53, 86, 108, 112, 147, 183, 256, 265, 267, 290

World Council of Churches Publications, 150 Route de Ferney, 1211 Geneva 2, ©1989 *With All God's People*, compiled by John Carden, copyright in prayers listed under originating publishers except: Prayer used in the Ecumenical Centre on the visit of Pope John Paul II, 1984; 4th Assembly, Caribbean Conference of Churches, 1986   14; Justice, Peace and Integrity of Creation women's workshop, Tonga, 1987   286; exact source unknown   72, 126, 247, 257, 268, 288

Yost, Mary, Associates, 59 East 54th Street, Suite 73, New York, NY 10022, © 1975, 77 Malcolm Boyd, *Am I Running With You, God?*   125, 191